D0713278

The Case of the Zodiac Killer

by Diane Yancey

LUCENT BOOKS
A part of Gale, Cengage Learning

GALE
CENGAGE Learning™

Detroit • New York • San Francisco • New Haven, Conn • Waterville, Maine • London

LIBRARY OF CONGRESS CATALOGING-IN-PUBLICATION DATA

Yancey, Diane.
  The case of the Zodiac Killer / by Diane Yancey.
    p. cm. — (Crime scene investigations)
  Includes bibliographical references and index.
  ISBN 978-1-4205-0063-9 (hardcover)
1. Serial murder investigation—United States—Case studies—Juvenile
literature. 2. Serial murders—United States—Case studies—Juvenile literature.
3. Serial murderers—United States—Biography—Juvenile literature. I. Title.
  HV8079.H6.C347 2008
  364.152'30973—dc22

                                                                    2008006163

Lucent Books
27500 Drake Rd
Farmington Hills MI 48331

ISBN-13: 978-1-4205-0063-9
ISBN-10: 1-4205-0063-5

Printed in the United States of America
1 2 3 4 5 6 7 12 11 10 09 08

Contents

Foreword

The popularity of crime scene and investigative crime shows on television has come as a surprise to many who work in the field. The main surprise is the concept that crime scene analysts are the true crime solvers, when in truth, it takes dozens of people, doing many different jobs, to solve a crime. Often, the crime scene analyst's contribution is a small one. One Minnesota forensic scientist says that the public "has gotten the wrong idea. Because I work in a lab similar to the ones on *CSI*, people seem to think I'm solving crimes left and right—just me and my microscope. They don't believe me when I tell them that it's just the investigators that are solving crimes, not me."

Crime scene analysts do have an important role to play, however. Science has rapidly added a whole new dimension to gathering and assessing evidence. Modern crime labs can match a hair of a murder suspect to one found on a murder victim, for example, or recover a latent fingerprint from a threatening letter, or use a powerful microscope to match tool marks made during the wiring of an explosive device to a tool in a suspect's possession.

Probably the most exciting of the forensic scientist's tools is DNA analysis. DNA can be found in just one drop of blood, a dribble of saliva on a toothbrush, or even the residue from a fingerprint. Some DNA analysis techniques enable scientists to tell with certainty, for example, whether a drop of blood on a suspect's shirt is that of a murder victim.

While these exciting techniques are now an essential part of many investigations, they cannot solve crimes alone. "DNA doesn't come with a name and address on it," says the Minnesota forensic scientist. "It's great if you have someone in custody to match the sample to, but otherwise, it doesn't help.

That's the investigator's job. We can have all the great DNA evidence in the world, and without a suspect, it will just sit on a shelf. We've all seen cases with very little forensic evidence get solved by the resourcefulness of a detective."

While forensic specialists get the most media attention today, the work of detectives still forms the core of most criminal investigations. Their job, in many ways, has changed little over the years. Most cases are still solved through the persistence and determination of a criminal detective whose work may be anything but glamorous. Many cases require routine, even mind-numbing tasks. After the July 2005 bombings in London, for example, police officers sat in front of video players watching thousands of hours of closed-circuit television tape from security cameras throughout the city, and as a result were able to get the first images of the bombers.

The Lucent Books Crime Scene Investigations series explores the variety of ways crimes are solved. Titles cover particular crimes such as murder, specific cases such as the killing of three civil rights workers in Mississippi, or the role specialists such as medical examiners play in solving crimes. Each title in the series demonstrates the ways a crime may be solved, from the various applications of forensic science and technology to the reasoning of investigators. Sidebars examine both the limits and possibilities of the new technologies and present crime statistics, career information, and step-by-step explanations of scientific and legal processes.

The Crime Scene Investigations series strives to be both informative and realistic about how members of law enforcement—criminal investigators, forensic scientists, and others—solve crimes, for it is essential that student researchers understand that crime solving is rarely quick or easy. Many factors—from a detective's dogged pursuit of one tenuous lead to a suspect's careless mistakes to sheer luck to complex calculations computed in the lab—are all part of crime solving today.

"This Is the Zodiac Speaking"

In the late 1960s, San Francisco was a city in turmoil, troubled by anger, rebellion, and public unrest. Thousands of young people, who were part of the youth counterculture movement known as the hippies, flocked the streets, outraging ordinary citizens with their preoccupation with drugs, promiscuous sex, and pacifism. Disillusioned college students publicly burned their draft cards, staged strikes on campuses, and clashed with police over the unpopular Vietnam War. The Black Panthers, angry young African Americans who were tired of discrimination, pushed for civil rights, even at the price of violence.

The Black Panthers and their push for civil rights was just one of the movements going on in San Francisco when the Zodiac killer first appeared.

A Turbulent Decade

When the Zodiac struck in 1968, Bay Area police were already distracted by events that threatened to overwhelm their law enforcement capabilities. Journalist Duffy Jennings explains in the article "Zodiac vs. the Chron City Desk" published in the San Francisco Chronicle.

As big as the Zodiac story was, it came at the dawn of an extraordinary decade in the crime annals of Northern California, the first in a rapid-fire succession of major events that rocked the Bay Area between 1969 and 1979.

The short list included the shocking Patty Hearst kidnapping, Hibernia bank robbery, Symbionese Liberation Army manhunt and L.A. shootout; the random Zebra murders on the streets of San Francisco; the San Rafael courthouse shootout and murder of Judge Harold Haley; the Golden Dragon restaurant massacre in Chinatown; the mass murder and suicides of more than 900 people—most from the Bay Area—in Jonestown, Guyana . . . the City Hall assassinations of Mayor George Moscone and Supervisor Harvey Milk; and the subsequent murder trial of Supervisor Dan White and its riotous aftermath.

Hardened reporters, including combat veterans and others who had seen more than their share of human tragedy, marveled at the relentless magnitude of it all and wondered what else could possibly happen next.

Duffy Jennings, "Zodiac vs. the Chron City Desk," *San Francisco Chronicle*, February 25, 2007. http://sfgate.com/cgi-bin/article.cgi?f=/c/a/2007/02/25/PKGANO4TRFI.DTL.

The tension was heightened in 1968 by the appearance of a mysterious killer named the Zodiac. He was a shadowy individual who struck randomly, vanished quickly, and bragged about his exploits in coded messages and letters that opened with the arrogant phrase "This is the Zodiac speaking."[1]

At first he seemed to menace only young couples parked in lonely spots after dark. Later attacks, and his threats to kill children and others, however, quickly spread fear throughout the San Francisco Bay Area, a region of over 4.5 million people. "People were terrified," explained Jean Donaldson of the Napa County sheriff's office. "The killings . . . occurred in so many different areas and jurisdictions that there was an impression that it could happen anywhere."[2]

Puzzled and Frustrated

As the number of Zodiac victims climbed, Bay Area police searched full time for the killer. They collected and analyzed data, interviewed surviving victims, and checked out thousands of suspects. They uncovered tantalizing evidence, but nothing that definitely pointed to the killer.

Inevitably, disagreements arose over who the police should be looking for. Some insisted that the killer was a psychopath—a person with a mental disorder characterized by antisocial and criminal behavior—who got sexual gratification by murdering his victims. Others pointed to his interest in astrological signs, maps, and cryptograms and maintained that police should be on the lookout for someone who was motivated by witchcraft or the occult. In the meantime, the Zodiac remained at large, building a reputation as a super criminal who avoided capture due to his superior intellect.

Then, suddenly, the killings stopped. The Zodiac continued to send his cryptic messages for a time, but eventually they, too, came to an end. Investigators were left puzzled and frustrated. They knew that serial killers seldom stop killing, and the Zodiac had announced in his November 9, 1969, letter that he was going to change his method of

What Is in a Name?

The Zodiac killer never explained why he chose his alias. Some popular theories are as follows:

1 He was involved in astrology. Some professional astrologers see evidence of this in the timing of the Zodiac murders and the dates letters arrived. Author Robert Graysmith points out that some of the Zodiac's code symbols were taken from the fifteenth-century zodiac alphabet.

2 He was inspired by Ford car called the Zodiac, produced in the 1960s. The car had a crossed-circle hood ornament.

3 He was a fan of the singing group Maurice Williams and the Zodiacs, active in the late 1950s and early 1960s.

4 He admired and/or possessed a Zodiac brand watch. The brand was notable for the crossed-circle symbol on its face.

One theory as to how the Zodiac killer chose his name was that he was a fan of the musical group, Maurice Williams and the Zodiacs (pictured).

operating (MO) so that deaths would look like accidents or robberies gone wrong. Investigators feared they were overlooking his crimes, but there was also the possibility that he had died, moved out of the area, or been imprisoned for some other crime.

With no definite answers, police could only review the evidence, investigate new tips that came in, and hope that the killer would one day be revealed. Developments in scientific technology in the 1990s offered new hope of cracking the case. Forensic DNA consultant Norah Rudin observed, "DNA analysis is having a huge effect. You see reports every day of cold cases being reinvestigated and answers gotten in cases that previously had no hope of being solved."[3] But even DNA did not give investigators of the Zodiac case the results for which they hoped.

"Like the Boogey Man"

A classic in the history of serial murder, the Zodiac case remains unsolved and continues to attract professional and amateur detectives. "I think [the Zodiac is] a mystery. It's comparable to Jack the Ripper. . . . They don't know who did it. They don't know much. He's like the Boogey Man. . . . He attacks people for no reason,"[4] states former San Francisco police detective Michael Maloney.

The case is compelling for more than its mysterious elements, however. It is a story of young, innocent victims who died horribly. It is an example of investigators who become obsessed with catching a brutal killer. More importantly, however, it is the account of a master terrorist who knew how to play on human fears to bolster his ego, achieve control, and gain fame. "There was sheer panic back then," says author and San Francisco resident Robert Graysmith. "Obviously, he was a very intelligent man. He used different weapons each time. He seemed to know the comings and goings of the police. He knew chemistry and astronomy and horoscopes. It was nothing like anyone had come up against before. It was frightening. I was frightened."[5]

Good-bye, Young Lovers

The Zodiac claimed to have murdered thirty-seven people in the course of his killing spree, but police identified only seven who they could confirm were victims of his knife and gun. Five of those victims died. All were young. All were attacked without warning, most while they sat in their cars. Violence was the last thing on their minds, as surviving victim Bryan Hartnell emphasized. "It was nothing but pure shock. . . . I just did not expect it. I just didn't expect that he would do that [stab me]. That was a variable I had completely left out."[6]

David and Betty Lou

The first confirmed Zodiac attack took place on December 29, 1968, on Lake Herman Road near Benicia, California. Benicia is a small town about 24 miles (39km) from San Francisco.

The Zodiac killer targeted his victims in the San Francisco area.

Becoming a Police Officer

Job Description:
Police officers perform general law enforcement tasks, including patrolling an assigned district and responding to calls for service. They may issue traffic citations, direct traffic at the scene of an accident, investigate a burglary, or give first aid to an accident victim. The job can be hazardous and often involves working in the middle of the night or early morning.

Education:
Aspiring police officers must obtain a high school diploma or general educational development (GED) credential. They must then complete either a two-year associate's program or a four-year bachelor's program in a criminal justice–related field before applying to a law enforcement agency.

Police recruits undergo training for twelve to fourteen weeks at a police academy. Training includes classroom instruction in constitutional law and civil rights, state laws and local ordinances, and accident investigation. Recruits also receive instruction in patrol, traffic control, firearms usage, self-defense, first aid, and emergency response.

Qualifications:
Aspiring police recruits must pass several prehiring exams, including a civil service test, drug tests, psychological tests, and physical exams. Physical fitness is a plus, as are good communication skills.

Salary:
$25,000 to $68,000 per year

On the night of the twenty-ninth, sixteen-year-old Betty Lou Jensen told her parents that she and her boyfriend, seventeen-year-old David Faraday, were going to a concert.

In fact, Faraday had something more than music on his mind. A schoolmate named Sharon remembers, "David called me and told me that he was going to ask her [Betty Lou] to go steady with him. Then he asked me if I thought she would accept. Of course I said yes; she liked him an awful lot. He was going to give her a ring. He asked me where they could go to be alone. Everybody used to park at St. Catherine's Hill and get run off by the police. He didn't want to go there and asked me where else they could go to be alone."[7]

Faraday and Jensen decided to drive into the country along Lake Herman Road. Just after 10 P.M., Faraday parked his brown and beige Rambler station wagon on a graveled turnout near the lake's pumping station. The spot was isolated, so the couple locked all the doors. Jensen then slid over on the car's bench seat so she was sitting close to Faraday.

"So Much Blood"

An hour later, when Stella Borges Medeiros drove down Lake Herman Road on her way into town, her car's headlights lit up a heart-stopping scene. Two bodies lay beside the road. The Rambler's rear window was shattered, and the passenger door was open. Faraday lay just to the right of the car, fatally wounded. Police later noted that he had the class ring he planned to give Jensen in his left hand.

Jensen lay about 10 feet (3m) away and was already dead. "I never saw so much blood on the side of the road in my life,"[8] said one of the ambulance attendants who responded to Medeiros's call. Faraday died en route to the hospital. After a search of the area, investigators determined that someone using .22-caliber ammunition had come up on foot behind the car and shot out the right rear window and the left rear tire. The tactic had driven the teens from the car. Jensen had scrambled out of the passenger door and started to run for the road when her attacker shot her five times in the back. Faraday exited the car on the right side, too, and was shot at close range in the head.

Benicia residents were shocked by the murders, and students at the victims' high schools offered a reward for the capture of the killer. Police believed he was probably one of the couple's friends or acquaintances and slanted their investigation in that direction. Sharon recalled, "At one time police thought the killer was some guy who used to like Betty Lou. His name was Richard. . . . They went after him full force. They said he did it, that it was jealousy. He came over to my house one day and just cried to my mother. He was so scared."[9]

Mike and Darlene

The Jensen/Faraday case was still open and unsolved on the night of July 4, 1969. At that time, another assault on a young couple took place on the eastern outskirts of Vallejo, California, just a few miles from the Jensen/Faraday attack.

Darlene Ferrin was a twenty-two-year-old married waitress, who enjoyed dating other men. About 11:30 P.M., she picked up a friend, nineteen-year-old Michael Mageau, in front of his home. The two drove Ferrin's brown Chevrolet Corvair to a parking lot in nearby Blue Rock Springs Park, where they parked and sat talking.

Like this scene still from the Zodiac *film shows, the killer pulled up to Ferrin's rear bumper and shone a flashlight into the faces of Ferrin and Mageau.*

Shortly before midnight, a brown car—possibly a 1958 or 1959 Ford Falcon—pulled up beside the couple. The car idled there a moment, then drove rapidly away. Five minutes later it returned and stopped close by their rear bumper. The driver, a lone male, got out and walked toward them, holding a bright flashlight so it shone directly in their faces.

Attacked!

Mageau assumed the newcomer was a policeman and reached for his driver's license. Without saying a word, however, the man raised a gun and fired five 9mm bullets through the passenger-side window. The bullets hit Mageau in the face and body, passed through him, and hit Ferrin. Her efforts to avoid them were hampered by the steering wheel, but Mageau scrambled into the back seat. In so doing, he was hit in the knee by another bullet. The stranger kept shooting, now concentrating on Ferrin. She was struck in each arm and in her right side as she tried to squirm out of the way.

Then abruptly, the shooter stopped and turned to walk away. In a haze of pain, Mageau shifted in the back seat and let out an agonized cry. The sound caused the shooter to pause. He returned to the wounded couple, where he wordlessly fired two more rounds into them. He then went back to his own car and drove away.

Despite his pain, Mageau opened the car door and rolled out onto the pavement. There, three teens discovered him and called the police. When help arrived, Mageau managed to gasp out a few words. "A white man . . . drive up . . . in a car . . . got out . . . walked up to the car, shined flashlight inside . . . started shooting."[10]

Mageau and Ferrin were loaded into an ambulance and taken to a nearby hospital, where Ferrin, who had been shot a total of five times, was pronounced dead on arrival. Mageau was placed in the intensive care unit in critical condition. He ultimately survived.

"I Want to Report a Double Murder"

While doctors worked to save Mageau's life, the Vallejo Police Department received an unexpected phone call. A man who spoke in a flat voice with no trace of an accent stated, "I want to report a double murder. If you will go 1 mile east on Columbus Parkway to the public park you will find the kids in a brown car. They were shot with a 9 mil. Luger. I also killed those kids last year. Good-bye."[11] The receptionist noted that the caller's voice deepened and became taunting on the last words.

Police traced the call to a pay phone located a few blocks away from the Vallejo Sheriff's Department. No evidence was found at the booth, although an eyewitness testified that he had seen a man in a brown car using the phone at 12:40 AM, a half hour after the attack.

With the anonymous call a dead end, police began investigating possible suspects. They included Ferrin's husband and several other men she had known. The anonymous call continued to trouble police, however. It gave them the first hint that they were dealing with a vicious killer, who had killed before and might kill again.

Bryan and Cecelia

The killer had identified himself by name—the Zodiac—by the time another young couple was attacked on September 27, 1969, on the shores of Lake Berryessa in Napa County. The lake lay just 30 miles (48km) northeast of Vallejo, close enough to the Bay Area that residents could drive to its shores on weekends for a few hours of sun and recreation.

Twenty-two-year-old Cecelia Shepard and twenty-year-old Bryan Hartnell were friends who had both attended Pacific Union College (PUC), located in the small town of Angwin near Berryessa. Shepard was transferring to the University of California at Riverside to study music, however. On September 27, her last day at PUC, she and Hartnell made the short drive to Berryessa for a final good-bye talk.

Hartnell parked his white Volkswagen Karmann Ghia near the western shore of the lake, and the two walked out onto a

Cecelia Shepard (pictured) and Bryan Hartnell were attacked on September 27, 1969 on the shores of Lake Berryessa.

small peninsula of land. There they spread a blanket under the trees. Hartnell remembered, "It was really beautiful out there. . . . I lay down on my back and she lay down on her stomach, you know, kind of resting her head on my shoulder, and we were talking, kind of reminiscing about old times, and stuff."[12]

Hooded Killer

The spot was somewhat remote, but it was only 4:00 P.M. when they arrived, and both felt perfectly safe. Sometime around 6 P.M., however, Hartnell heard a noise behind him and asked Shepard, who was facing that way, what it was. She looked and saw a man standing behind a tree. A few seconds later, Hartnell heard her exclaim, "Oh my God, he has a gun!"[13]

Call from a Killer

The Zodiac not only made an anonymous call taking credit for the Ferrin/Mageau attack, but he also claimed responsibility by phone for the Shepard/Hartnell attack. At 7:40 P.M. on September 27, 1969, he called the Napa Police Department switchboard. The operator heard a voice state calmly, "I want to report a murder, no, a double murder. They are two miles north of Park Headquarters. They were in a white Volkswagen Karmen-Ghia." When the operator asked "Where are you now?" the caller answered "I'm the one that did it." The phone was put down, not hung up.

Police were not quick enough to catch the Zodiac that night, but they consoled themselves at the thought that he was not infallible. He believed he had killed Hartnell and he had not. If he had made one mistake, it was likely he would make more. Then they would catch him.

D. Slaight, "Napa Police Department Supplementary Report," September 27, 1969. Zodiackiller.com. www.zodiackiller.com/LBReport32.html.

The man not only had a gun, but also a black cloth hood covering his face and extending over his chest. The hood was flat and rectangular, like a paper bag on top. A white crossed-circle symbol was stitched across the chest. The man's eyes were hidden by a pair of clip-on sunglasses. He also had a foot-long (0.3m) knife in a riveted sheath hanging at his waist.

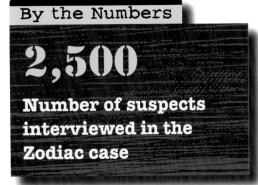

By the Numbers

2,500

Number of suspects interviewed in the Zodiac case

As the intruder approached, he pointed the gun at the couple, explaining that he had just escaped from prison and needed money and a car. Hartnell thought the incident was just a robbery, and was not alarmed when the intruder ordered him and Shepard to lie down. Shepard was ordered to tie Hartnell's hands behind his back, then the stranger tied Shepard's.

"He Was Killing Me"

Hartnell had no money on him, but, in an attempt to maintain friendly relations with the stranger, he offered to help in some other way. The stranger refused. Then, without warning, the stranger swiftly drew his knife and began plunging it viciously and repeatedly into Hartnell's back. Hartnell tried to describe the scene: "CHOMP, CHOMP, CHOMP, CHOMP . . . you know, that kind of sound . . . and Cecelia turned to see . . . and she just about fainted. She went hysterical."[14] Rather than try to fight, Hartnell lay still. "I didn't holler, I didn't move. I was just waiting for him to finish—for it to be over. He was killing me."[15]

Worked into a frenzy, the stranger turned from Hartnell to Shepard, who was writhing and screaming. Furiously, he stabbed her over and over in the back, chest, side, and lower abdomen.

Then, just as abruptly as he started, he stood up and walked away. Hartnell estimated that the attack had lasted about fifteen minutes. He struggled to his feet and called to a couple in a boat just offshore, asking for help. They indicated they would go for a park ranger. Hartnell then tried to walk to his car.

Hartnell was repeatedly attacked with a knife, but he survived.

Finally a passerby in a pickup truck stopped to help, and shortly thereafter, an ambulance and the police arrived. Shepard died within two days of the stabbing, but Hartnell survived and was able to give a rough description of their attacker.

Paul Stine

Two weeks later, the killer struck again. This time he changed his method of operation and targeted a single person instead of a couple. Twenty-nine-year-old Paul Lee Stine was working as a cab driver while studying for his PhD at San Francisco State College. On the evening of October 11, 1969, he was driving in downtown San Francisco, en route to pick up a customer. According to his records, somewhere along the way, he stopped to pick up another fare. This unknown individual got in the front seat and directed Stine to drive to Washington and Maple streets. On arrival, Stine pulled to the curb. Instead of paying him, however, the passenger shot him, point-blank, in the right side of the head with a 9mm semiautomatic revolver.

Paul Lee Stine was working as a cab driver when he was attacked by the killer. This was the first time the killer had attacked a single person instead of a couple.

Death of "a Small-Town Guy"

To the public, Paul Stine was a cab driver, notable only because he was a victim of the Zodiac. To his family and friends, however, he was much more, as journalist Christopher Caskey reports in the article "Valley Rocked After Hughson Grad Became Zodiac Victim," published in the Modesto Bee.

Paul Stine was a small-town guy taking a crack at life in the big city. In high school, he'd been the boy voted "most likely to succeed." . . .

He attended Hughson High School, graduating in 1957, . . . nicknamed "Einstein" by his classmates. He was a member of numerous campus organizations, including student court and the school newspaper.

After high school, Stine went to Fresno State College. At the time of his death, he was working the night shift driving a taxicab while studying for a graduate degree in philosophy at San Francisco State College. . . . "He was a hell of a scholar," said [former roommate William] Strangio, who lives in Corvallis, Oregon. "His big deal was to write the great American novel."

Christopher Caskey, "Valley Rocked After Hughson Grad Became Zodiac Victim," *Modesto Bee*, March 2, 2007.

Although he risked being caught, the killer lingered around the cab for a time. He rifled through Stine's pockets, taking his wallet and keys. He then used a cloth to wipe down the interior of the cab. Getting out, he left Stine sprawled across the front seat while he wiped down the passenger door. He then walked around the cab and wiped the driver doors before walking away northward toward the Presidio, a large nearby park.

Three teens witnessed the crime from a house across the street and called the police. An ambulance quickly responded, but it was too late for Stine. Police called in seven dog teams and instituted a search of the area where the killer was last seen, but he was not found. Homicide detectives viewed the incident as a robbery gone wrong until three days later, on October 14, when the *San Francisco Chronicle* received a letter from the Zodiac, who took credit for the killing.

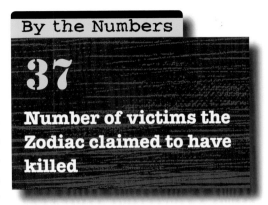

By the Numbers

37

Number of victims the Zodiac claimed to have killed

Robert and Linda

Articles about the murders, published in California newspapers, generated widespread interest in the Zodiac. As a result, police in other towns reviewed their files to see if they contained similar unsolved cases that fit the killer's MO. Several came to light, dating as far back as 1963.

The first unsolved case was the murder of eighteen-year-old Robert Domingos and seventeen-year-old Linda Edwards. On June 4, 1963, the two teens—seniors at Lompoc High School, about 300 miles (483km) south of San Francisco—had gone to the beach to sunbathe. The spot they chose was isolated, and there the killer attacked them. The couple tried to escape, but, as they ran, the killer shot them in the back. Domingos was hit eleven times and Edwards nine. The weapon used was a .22-caliber semiautomatic. The killer then dragged the bodies to a nearby shack that was hidden among a grove of trees and attempted to set the shack on fire.

The couple was found the next day, and the crime scene was thoroughly investigated. The Santa Barbara County Sheriff's Department was still looking for the killer in 1969, when they realized the MO of their crime was similar to the Zodiac's.

The attack had been on a teenage couple in a remote location. Domingos' hands had been bound. There was no apparent motive for the assault. Sheriff John Carpenter stated, "We are not using the notoriety of the Zodiac to dispose of a difficult case, nor are we closing our minds to the possibility that he may not be responsible. Very simply, this office feels that sufficient evidence exists to warrant further investigation."[16]

Cheri Jo Bates

Another possible Zodiac murder was that of Cheri Jo Bates, an eighteen-year-old Riverside Community College (RCC) student. Riverside lies almost 450 miles (724km) south of San Francisco. At approximately 6:00 P.M. on October 30, 1966, Bates had gone to the college library to pick up some books, then returned to her car. In the meantime, the killer had tampered with her vehicle so that it would not start.

No one knows exactly what took place in the next few hours. Footprints in the dust showed that the two walked about 600 feet (183m) to a driveway that ran between two houses. There, the killer attacked Bates with a knife, stabbing her four times in the chest and back and slashing her throat almost to the bone. She was also beaten and choked. When police found her body the next day, they noted that she had not been sexually assaulted or robbed. Because they judged that Bates had talked with her attacker for almost an hour before she was killed, they guessed that he was a friend or acquaintance.

A month later, the case took an odd twist when the Riverside *Press-Enterprise* newspaper received a typed anonymous confession to Bates's murder. It was carefully prepared, however, so it was impossible to trace. In December 1966, a custodian at RCC discovered a morbid poem that seemed to describe Bates's death carved on the underside of a library desk. On April 30, 1967, letters were mailed to the *Press-Enterprise*, Riverside police, and Cheri's father, all stating that Bates had had to die and that more would be killed. No one had heard of the Zodiac in 1967, however, so a possible connection was not considered until after October 1969.

Kathleen Johns

Once the Zodiac became an acknowledged threat, incidences occurred that made investigators think he continued to hunt for victims after Stine's murder. The kidnapping of Kathleen Johns on March 22, 1970, did not fit his MO, but several aspects of the case made it likely that it involved the infamous killer.

Early in the evening on the twenty-second, twenty-three-year-old Johns left San Bernardino, about 10 miles (16km) north of Riverside, and began driving north with her ten-month-old daughter to visit her mother in the town of Petaluma, California. Around midnight, a driver in a light-colored car began honking and flashing his lights, then pulled alongside her and yelled that her rear tire was wobbling. Johns pulled over and allowed him to fix the tire. When she steered back onto the highway, however, the entire wheel fell off. The stranger then offered to drive her to a nearby service station just down the road. He looked and acted reliable, so Johns gathered up her small daughter and got in his car.

Rather than going to the service station, however, the man left the highway and, for two hours, drove Johns along desolate back roads, ignoring her panicky demands to be released. Finally, when he stopped at an intersection, Johns leaped from the car holding her daughter and fled into a nearby field.

The Zodiac sent letters to the San Francisco Chronicle *letting them know where to look for clues to his crimes.*

The driver waited for a few minutes and then drove away. Johns made her way to the Petaluma Police Department, where she saw a composite sketch of the Zodiac and immediately identified him as the man who had kidnapped her. When police went to retrieve her car the next day, they found that it had been set on fire and was entirely destroyed.

Johns's near-hysterical condition when she arrived in Petaluma caused some investigators to suspect that she had identified the Zodiac only because she saw his sketch prominently displayed in the police station. However, the *San Francisco Chronicle* received a letter, mailed on July 24, 1970, that read: "I have a little list, starting with that woeman + her baby that I gave a rather interesting ride for a coupple howers one evening a few months back that ended in my burning her car where I found them."[17] The details seemed to confirm Johns's identification. Still, some were doubtful. They pointed out that the Zodiac could have read about the incident in an area newspaper and then taken credit for it to enhance his reputation.

Donna Lass

There is no physical evidence to prove that Donna Lass was a Zodiac victim, but her disappearance in September 1970 is also blamed on the killer. Lass, a twenty-five-year-old nurse who was working at South Lake Tahoe, vanished on the afternoon of September 6. At about the same time, an unidentified male called her employer, telling him that Lass would be absent due to a family illness. When police later checked with the family, however, they discovered that the call was a hoax.

Lass had not been found when, on March 22, 1971, a postcard arrived at the *San Francisco Chronicle*, addressed to the attention of "Paul Averly.". Paul Avery was a journalist who had received a letter from the Zodiac in October 1970, and the killer had misspelled his name in exactly the same way. The card was covered with cutouts of pictures and phrases such as "sought victim 12," "peek through the pines," and "pass Lake Tahoe areas."[18] Its return address was simply "The Zodiac," coupled

Timeline of Zodiac-related Crimes				
Date of Crime	Victim(s)	City in California where crime was committed	Method used in crime	Confirmed by police as a Zodiac murder?
June 4, 1963	Linda Edwards and Robert Domingos	Lompoc area	Gunshot (.22 caliber semi-automatic)	Investigated but never confirmed
October 30, 1966	Cheri Jo Bates	Riverside	Stabbing, strangulation and physical assault	Investigated but never confirmed
December 29, 1968	Betty Lou Jensen and David Faraday	Benicia	Gunshot (.22-caliber)	Yes
July 4, 1969	Darlene Ferrin and Michael Mageau (he survived)	Vallejo	Gunshot (9mm)	Yes
September 27, 1969	Cecelia Shepard and Bryan Hartnell (he survived)	Lake Berryessa (in Napa County)	Stabbing (12-inch knife)	Yes
October 11, 1969	Paul Lee Stine	San Francisco	Gunshot (9mm semi-automatic revolver)	Yes
March 22, 1970	Kathleen Johns and her infant daughter (both survived)	Petaluma	Kidnapping	Investigated but never confirmed
September, 1970	Donna Lass	South Lake Tahoe area	Possible kidnapping/murder (victim never found)	Investigated but never confirmed

with a crossed-circle symbol. Documents examiner Sherman Morrill, the foremost handwriting expert in California at the time, studied the few inked words on the card and stated that they "conform and are consistent with all other [Zodiac] writings I have examined."[19] Based on that, investigators could not ignore the possible connection. Lass's body was never found.

Document examiners like Morrill played an important role in the Zodiac investigation. The killer communicated regularly through letters to the press and public. At times, it seemed like the letters were even more important to him than his killings. Profiler Gregg O. McCrary observed, "He especially enjoyed controlling the newspapers and the police agencies of a town the size of San Francisco. . . . Each day that went by without them catching him reinforced this opinion and sense of superiority. Every communication he sent fueled that fire."[20]

CHAPTER 2

Taunts from the Killer

The Zodiac was more than a serial killer; he was a master communicator who spread fear with a stroke of his felt-tip pen. For instance, after his attack on Shepard and Hartnell, he scrawled his distinctive crossed-circle symbol on the passenger door of Hartnell's car. The symbol was followed by the message:

> Vallejo
> 12–20–68
> 7–4–69
> Sept. 27, 69—6:30
> by knife.[21]

The dates were chilling reminders of his earlier attacks on young couples. Author Michael D. Kelleher says, "It was essentially snubbing his nose at law enforcement. And basically, telling others that, 'hey, I've been here. I can do what I want. I can do it as often as I want and there's nothing you can do about it.'"[22]

Letters and cipher messages were the killer's preferred form of communication. Cipher messages are secret messages written in code using characters or symbols. These messages often made front-page news, enthralling and terrifying Californians up and down the state. Kelleher notes, "Zodiac was a master manipulator of getting his cryptic little messages on the front pages of at least three different newspapers almost simultaneously."[23]

Three Letters, One Message

The first messages from the Zodiac arrived about two weeks after the attack on Ferrin and Mageau. On August 1, 1969, the *San Francisco Chronicle* received a letter that read in part: "Dear Editor This is the murderer of the 2 teenagers last Christmass at Lake Herman & the girl on the 4th of July near the golf course in Vallejo."[24]

Virtually identical letters were delivered to the San Francisco *Examiner* and the Vallejo *Times-Herald*. They all included facts about the attacks that only an eyewitness would know, including the brand of ammunition used, the exact position of the bodies, and the fact that Mageau had been shot in the knee. The letters were unsigned except for a crossed-circle symbol.

Handwritten letters from the Zodiac began to arrive soon after the attacks on Ferrin and Mageau.

Included with each letter was a handwritten cipher. The author threatened dire consequences if it was not published. "If you do not print this cipher, . . . I will cruise around all weekend killing lone people in the night . . . until I end up with a dozen,"[25] he wrote. Unwilling to call his bluff, San Francisco papers printed the cipher within the next few days.

The Hoax

San Francisco attorney Melvin Belli was the most celebrated Californian to become involved in the Zodiac case. Belli was known as the King of Torts for the many personal injury cases he won and for his defense of clients such as boxer Muhammad Ali and alleged assassin Jack Ruby. After winning a case, Belli regularly raised a Jolly Roger, a pirate's flag with skull and crossbones, over his office building and fired an antique cannon from the roof to announce his victory.

In October 1969 Oakland, California, police took an anonymous call from someone who claimed to be the Zodiac and asked to speak to Belli or attorney F. Lee Bailey. "I want one or the other to appear on the Channel Seven [TV] talk show. I'll make contact by telephone," the caller said. Belli readily agreed to appear, and at

One of America's most celebrated trial lawyers, Melvin Belli, became involved in the Zodiac case.

7:10 A.M., the caller, who wanted to be known as "Sam," phoned in.

At the end of several talk-filled hours, Belli set up a meeting with Sam, complete with police and television, radio, and newspaper reporters standing by. Sam never showed up, however, nor did he turn out to be the Zodiac. The calls were eventually traced to a mental patient incarcerated at Napa State Hospital.

Robert Graysmith, *Zodiac*. New York: Berkeley Books, 1986, p. 114.

Hard Proof

On August 4, 1969, the Zodiac sent another letter to the *Times-Herald*. This time he began with the phrase "This is the Zodiac speaking" and gave more details about earlier attacks. He described a witness—a shabbily dressed black man near the pay phone—who had given the police information about the car he drove.

By the Numbers

5

Number of confirmed Zodiac victims

He also explained how he had been able to pinpoint his victims in the dark. He had attached a flashlight to the barrel of his gun. "All I had to do was spray them as if it was a water hose,"[26] he explained. His information matched actual facts, so on that basis police concluded that the August 1 and August 4 letters were authentic.

They concluded the October 14 letter was authentic on even better evidence. In it, the Zodiac wrote, "I am the murderer of the taxi driver over by Washington St + Maple St last night, to prove this here is a blood stained piece of his shirt."[27] A swatch of Stine's shirt, stiff with blood, was enclosed with the letter. San Francisco police detective David Toschi noted, "With the matching of the shirt, we [were] pretty definitely up to our ears in the Zodiac murders."[28]

"School Children Make Nice Targets"

In addition to establishing a record of his kills, the Zodiac used his messages to ridicule police for their inability to catch him. In the October 14 letter he claimed he had been hiding in the Presidio, laughing as the police searched the area. "The S.F. Police could have caught me last night if they had searched the park properly instead of holding road races with their motorcicles seeing who could make the most noise,"[29] he said.

He also used his letters to make frightening threats. "School children make nice targets," he wrote. "I think I shall wipe out a school bus some morning. Just shoot out the frunt tire + then

Some Nice Zodiac Buttons

Custom lapel buttons have been popular since the 1800s, and in April 1970, the Zodiac sent a card to the Chronicle, *proposing that one be designed in his honor.*

I would like to see some nice Zodiac butons wandering around town. Every one else has these buttons, like, [peace sign], black power, Melvin eats blubber [reference to a pin that stated "Herman Melville Eats Blubber"], etc. Well it would cheer me up considerably if I saw a lot of people wearing my buton. Please no nasty ones like melvin's.

Thank you. ⊕

Dragon card, postmarked April 28, 1970. Zodiackiller.com. www.zodiackiller.com/DragonCard.html.

pick off the kiddies as they come bouncing out."[30] Before Stine's murder, police might have discounted the threat because the Zodiac had only attacked young couples. The murder of a single man in a populated section of town, however, indicated that the killer could change his MO. They had no guarantee that he would not change again and kill children.

Within hours, therefore, school officials were notified of the danger. Bus drivers were put on alert and children were instructed to get on the floor if shots were fired. In some districts, a police officer or volunteer rode on each bus. In others, police escorted buses along their routes while owners of small private planes shadowed routes from the air. Former Vallejo police officer Tony Pearsall recalled, "Zodiac said he was going to kill kids coming off a school bus so we got assigned to follow school buses for an hour or two every morning. And that went on for weeks."[31]

The Death Machine

Not content to scare school officials and parents, on November 8 and 9, 1969, the Zodiac sent two more messages and another piece of Stine's bloodstained shirt to the *Chronicle*. The first message was short and demanded that a new enclosed cipher be published. The second was a six-page letter. It repeated his taunts, claimed that the police would never catch him, and demanded again to have his messages published.

That letter also revealed a new threat. "If you cops think I'm going to take on a bus the way I stated I was, you deserve to have holes in your heads. . . . The death machine [bomb] is all ready made. I would have sent you pictures, but you would be nasty enough to trace them. . . . So I shall describe my masterpiece to you."[32] The description of the bomb was complete with detailed drawings. The letter concluded with a challenge: "What you do not know is whether the death machine is on sight [site] or whether it is being stored in my basement for future use. I think you do not have the man power to stop this one. . . . Have fun!"[33]

The Zodiac never planted his bomb, but he repeatedly threatened to do so. On April 20, 1970, for instance, he sent a letter to the *Chronicle*, enclosing a diagram of a bomb that differed from his earlier sketch. Eight days later, on April 28, 1970, he again demanded that details of his bomb be released to the public or he would blow up a busload of children.

Expert Scrutiny

Police realized that evidence found in and on the letters was their best link to the killer, so, as soon as they received one, they sent it for analysis to Morrill, who was head of the questioned documents section of California's Bureau of Criminal Identification and Investigation (BCII) in Sacramento. The BCII is under the Office of the Attorney General,

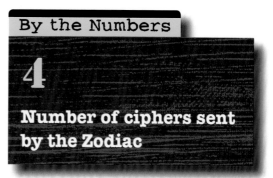

By the Numbers

4

Number of ciphers sent by the Zodiac

Morrill analyzed the paper and ink that the Zodiac killer used to try and track the killer. The Zodiac letters were written with blue felt tip pens, which were sold in most stores.

maintains the state's criminal history information, and provides criminal data and identification services to law enforcement. After 1980, the San Francisco Police Department employed its own forensic documents expert, Lloyd Cunningham, who studied the Zodiac letters, too.

After reading the letters, Morrill concluded the Zodiac was an educated man. In a 1970 letter he made references to *The Mikado*, a light opera written by W.S. Gilbert and Arthur Sullivan. He even seemed to know at least one of the songs by heart. Other factors reinforced Morrill's conclusion, too. "We know he deliberately misspells some words because he sometimes spells them correctly. His punctuation and paragraphing are perfect. His tenses and syntax [grammar] are perfect. His vocabulary is good."[34]

Determining that the Zodiac was educated was not the end of his analysis, however. Morrill knew that tracking down the source of the killer's paper and ink could help lead to his capture. Thus he scrutinized the paper on which the messages were written. It was always an inexpensive type and varied in size, as if it had been cut off a roll or sold in bulk. Zodiac's writing implements—blue felt-tip pens—were also common, sold in most stores. So were the cards he mailed. Detective Toschi explained, "We would check out all the greeting cards as Zodiac sent them just to see how common they were and how easy or difficult it would be for Zodiac to buy one. All the cards sent by Zodiac were common cards that could be purchased in any retail card store."[35]

The Tiniest Detail

In addition to analyzing paper and ink, Morrill studied the format of the messages. The Zodiac's margins were unusually straight and there was a good amount of space left between each line of words. His handwriting was relatively small and

What Can be Discovered from a Questioned Document?

1. The author of the document.
2. The origin of the document.
3. If more than one person created the document.
4. If the document is genuine or was altered.
5. Analysis of the materials used in producing the document
6. The age of the document.
7. Type of writing instrument or office machine used to create the document.

Taken from: National Association of Document Examiners. Available online at: http://documentexaminers.org/faq.html

cramped, a combination of cursive and printing. His lines of print usually slanted downward toward the right, but the flow of the letters across the page led Morrill to think the writer was comfortable when he was writing. He was not disguising his work in any way. Morrill stated, "I'm sure this is his natural hand printing, and he was used to using it a lot. It is so consistent."[36]

The writer of the letters also had several idiosyncrasies. For instance, he carefully crossed out his mistakes rather than rewriting his messages. He used a minimum of words to address his envelopes. He favored abbreviations such as "San Fran," "SF," and "Calif," and always included "Please Rush to Editor" somewhere on the envelope.

Finally, he formed certain letters the same way every time. Morrill noted that his lowercase r's always looked like checkmarks. His *d*'s seemed about to fall over on their sides, while his *K*'s were made with three strokes instead of two. The *t*'s were crossed low on the vertical. "His printing is distinctive,"[37] Morrill observed.

The Riverside Letters

In the process of analyzing the Zodiac's messages, Morrill also studied letters linked to Cheri Jo Bates's murder. These included copies of the confession, the poem carved into the desk, and the three notes, which stated tersely, "Bates had to die. There will be more."[38]

Morrill compared the Bates letters with known Zodiac letters and first noted obvious dissimilarities. The confession, for instance, had been typed on a portable Royal brand typewriter. Known Zodiac messages had been printed with felt-tip pen. The Bates letters were printed on binder paper. The Zodiac favored nonstandard size paper.

On the other hand, Morrill observed that the content and tone of the letters were similar to those written by the Zodiac. Also, the Bates letters had been hand printed, and that printing was consistent with the Zodiac's. The paper used was inexpensive. Morrill eventually determined that the Zodiac

Morrill compared the Zodiac letters with letters linked to the Bates murder. There were dissimilarities between the two, one being that the Bates confession was typed on a Royal brand typewriter.

had likely written them all. A reference in a later-confirmed Zodiac letter validated his determination. The killer wrote in March 1971: "I do have to give them [the police] credit for stumbling across my riverside activity, but they are only finding the easy ones."[39]

Sorting Out the Truth

In 1969 and 1970 the Zodiac gave Morrill plenty of material to analyze. In 1969 there were eight letters, ending with a Christmas card to noted San Francisco attorney Melvin Belli on December 20. It was authenticated by the inclusion of a piece of Stine's shirt. In the letter Zodiac begged Belli for help to prevent him from killing again. When Morrill analyzed the message, however, he pointed out that it was carefully composed, painstakingly printed, and showed no signs that the author was distressed and agitated. Morrill concluded that the killer was amusing himself at Belli's expense and/or seeking attention.

In 1970 the Zodiac sent six letters, the first two arriving at the *Chronicle* in April. One was a letter glorifying the killing of police. Another demanded that the public wear Zodiac buttons to commemorate his killings. On June 26, a letter included a cipher and map of the Bay Area with a nearby peak, Mount Diablo, marked with his crossed-circle symbol. The map

The Zodiac sent a Christmas card to San Francisco attorney Melvin Belli asking for his help.

coupled with the cipher allegedly indicated where he had planted his bomb. In that same letter he also claimed that he had shot a man sitting in a parked car with a .38-caliber weapon. Police investigated the claim, and determined that the only recent Bay Area shooting committed with a .38 involved San Francisco police officer Richard Radetich. His killer had been identified by an eyewitness and arrested, although he was later released for lack of evidence.

For a time, investigators wondered if they should add Radetich to their list of Zodiac victims, or assume that the Zodiac was taking credit for a murder he had not committed. They tentatively settled on the latter when they noticed that he had added a kind of scorecard to the end of his letters. With it, he gave a total of his victims compared to the police's success in capturing him. No new Zodiac murders were being discovered, but his total stood at twelve in June and jumped to thirty-seven in later messages. Police believed that he was bragging to feed his own ego and had simply used Radetich's death to swell his total.

Social Commentaries

After the Zodiac sent a letter to the *Los Angeles Times* in March 1971, taking credit for the Bates killing, he unexpectedly fell silent. Everyone waited and wondered if they

A Simple Cipher

Complex cipher systems are very difficult to master and decode, but a simple one is relatively easy to understand. FBI cryptanalyst Daniel Olson illustrates a basic substitution cipher.

A relatively basic form of substitution cipher is the Caesar Cipher, named for its Roman origins. The Caesar Cipher involves writing two alphabets, one above the other. The lower alphabet is shifted by one or more characters to the right or left and is used as the cipher text to represent the plain text letter in the alphabet above it.

Plain Text

A B C D E F G H I J **K** L M N O P Q R S T U V W X Y Z

B C D E F G H I J K **L** M N O P Q R S T U V W X Y Z A

Cipher Text

In this example, the plain text K is enciphered with the cipher text L. The phrase "Lucky Dog'" would be enciphered as follows:

Plain Text: L U C **K** Y D O G

Cipher Text: M V D **L** Z E P H

Daniel Olson, "Analysis of Criminal Codes and Ciphers," *Forensic Science Communication*, January 2000. www.fbi.gov/hq/lab/fsc/backissu/jan2000/olson.htm.

would hear from him again. They did beginning in 1974, but the new letters were so markedly different from early ones that some doubted he had written them. For instance, none began with the salutation "This is the Zodiac speaking."

None contained a cipher. None ended with the crossed-circle symbol.

In fact, with these letters, the Zodiac seemed to have changed to a social critic. On January 29, 1974, he praised the newly released movie, *The Exorcist* as great satirical comedy. On May 8, 1974, he protested advertisements for *Badlands*, a movie based on the murder spree of a young couple in Nebraska and Wyoming in the late 1950s. He called the film a glorification of murder and signed himself "A Citizen." Finally, on July 8, 1974, he criticized Marco Spinelli, a columnist for the *Chronicle*, claiming he had a serious psychological disorder. The letter was signed, "The Red Phantom (red with rage)." After receiving the letter, Spinelli left San Francisco for a period of retirement in Hawaii.

Despite the differences, Morrill and experts at the Federal Bureau of Investigation (FBI) crime laboratory judged the letters to be authentic based on their style, tone, and handwriting. The FBI wrote, "Inconsistencies are not sufficient to eliminate the writer of the Zodiac letters. . . . Similarities were noted which would indicate that [these letters] were probably prepared by the writer of the Zodiac letters."[40]

The Ciphers

The Zodiac's later letters did not include ciphers, but these puzzles were an integral part of his messages beginning in 1969 and continuing through June 1970. As everyone discovered, his ciphers were not simple substitutionary systems where one letter stood for another. Rather, he used more than fifty shapes and symbols to represent the twenty-six letters of the alphabet. Symbols included Greek letters, Morse code, navy semaphore (flag symbols), and astrological signs.

The Zodiac made it clear that the first three ciphers, which arrived with the first three letters in 1968, had to be combined to make one complete message. Police passed them on to naval cryptographers at Mare Island Naval Shipyard near Vallejo, but they had no success deciphering them. Then experts at

Donald G. Harden, a high school teacher, was able to solve the ciphers from the Zodiac.

the National Security Agency and the Central Intelligence Agency—government agencies experienced in cryptography and intelligence gathering—were tasked to help, but they were unsuccessful, too.

In the meantime, the ciphers had been published in northern California newspapers and had generated a great deal of interest. Donald G. Harden of Salinas, California, was one of the thousands who noticed them. Harden was a high school teacher with an interest in puzzles. He and his wife set to work to try and solve those from the Zodiac and, after almost twenty-four hours of inspiration and hard work, they succeeded. The message began with a frightening sentence: "I like killing people because it is so much fun it is more fun than killing wild game in the forrest because man is the most dangerous anamal of all to kill."[41] The Hardens notified the *Chronicle*, who passed the decoded message to Vallejo police. Navy cryptologists soon verified that it was indeed the solution to the riddle.

"The Most Dangerous Game"

With the solution in hand, investigators sat down and analyzed the importance of the cipher. They noted that the first sentence was essentially the Zodiac's mission statement, explaining why he murdered. The mention of man as a dangerous animal reminded them of a 1924 short story by Richard Connell titled "The Most Dangerous Game." In it, a deranged man named General Zaroff lures humans onto his private island where he

From the cipher, investigators believed that the Zodiac had either read or seen the film version of Richard Connell's short story, The Most Dangerous Game. *A scene from the 1932 film version is shown here.*

hunts them to the death. Zaroff states, "Here on my island I hunt the most dangerous game [humans]."[42]

The story was made into a movie in 1932 and again in 1945, and from the Zodiac's reference, investigators concluded that he had either read the story or seen one of the movies. Research indicated that the 1932 version had been shown in several Bay Area theaters in 1969, but the clue did not help them find the killer.

The cipher also stated the Zodiac's belief that after he died he would go to paradise, where those he killed would be his slaves. The philosophy provided more insight into his psychological makeup. Psychiatric experts at the California Medical Facility in Vacaville postulated, "He is probably a guy who broods about cut-off feelings, about being cut off from his fellow man. . . . He probably feels his fellow man looks down on him for some reason. The belief that his victims would be his slaves in an afterlife reflects a feeling of omnipotence [power] indicating a . . . delusion of grandeur."[43]

Locked Puzzles

Although the Hardens had successfully deciphered the first puzzles, they could not duplicate their success with later ones. These were included with letters on November 8, 1969; April 20, 1970; and June 26, 1970. April's was particularly attention

How to Create a Dictionary Code

1. Use a dictionary or any book with many different words.

2. Write down your message in English, this is called "plaintext."
   Example: YOU CAN CREATE YOUR OWN CODED MESSAGE.

3. Find the first word in your dictionary or book.

4. Write down the page number, column or paragraph number, and the Nth word down that column or into that paragraph.
   Example: YOU = Page 1454, Column 1, 24th word down.

5. Separate the numbers by a period.
   YOU = 1454.1.24

6. Repeat Steps 2-4 for every word in your sentence.
   YOU = 1454.1.24   CAN = 178.1.35   CREATE = 293.1.29
   YOUR = 1454.2.2   OWN = 887.1.16   CODED = 239.2.2D
   MESSAGE = 778.2.20

7. In some cases, you may have to add a prefix or suffix to the numbers.
   CODED = 239.2.2D

8. The finished cipher should look like the cipher below.
   1454.1.24 178.1.35 293.1.29 1454.2.2 887.1.16
   239.2.2D 778.2.20
   Remember to leave a space between each group of numbers.

grabbing, because in it the killer wrote, "My name is" followed by a set of thirteen symbols. Authors Michael D. Kelleher and David Van Nuys write, "The use of ciphers had . . . become a Zodiac trademark, and the killer knew it would capture the interest of those on the case, the media, and readers of local newspapers."[44]

Despite all the interest, none of the last three ciphers was ever solved. The Zodiac had complicated his coding process to the point that it was impossible to break, even for the most skilled cryptologists. Investigators were left wondering if genuine information had been included in the codes or not. Kelleher and Van Nuys state, "We can only guess at what the Zodiac was trying to communicate; and that is an unsure proposition with a man of his obvious penchant [fondness] for deceit and trickery."[45]

Hunting the Zodiac

Some considered the Zodiac's letters and codes intriguing, but his murders were simply brutal and terrifying. They lacked cleverness, skill, or subtlety. They horrified everyone by their savagery, their unexpectedness, and their futility. Psychologist and author David Van Nuys notes, "Zodiac was the prototypic [model] terrorist in terms of holding a large population captive. . . . He was very clever in being able to . . . [create] enormous fear that spread throughout the Bay Area."[46]

Driven by anger, investigators tirelessly pursued the killer. They processed each scene for evidence, interviewed witnesses, and tracked down leads. Some worked so hard that their health and personal lives were affected. Detective David Toschi, for instance, was hospitalized with a bleeding ulcer in 1982 after working the case for fourteen years. Napa County sheriff detective Kenneth Narlow remembers, "It was just heart wrenching to see what happened to those kids. I put my heart and soul into finding the Zodiac."[47]

Multiple Investigations

At least five law enforcement agencies worked on the Zodiac case, most at the same time. They included the Solano County Sheriff's Office, the Vallejo Police Department, the Napa County Sheriff's Office, the San Francisco Police Department, and the Riverside Police Department. The FBI did not directly investigate the case, but experts in its crime laboratory assisted in performing forensic examinations such as analysis of codes, handwriting, and fingerprints.

Detectives Les Lundblad and Russell Butterbach of the Solano County Sheriff's Office took the lead in investigating the

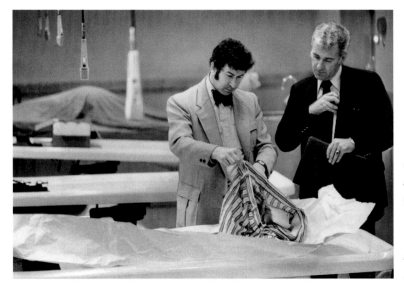

San Francisco homicide inspectors David Toschi, left, and William Armstrong headed up the Zodiac Squad.

Jensen/Faraday murders. Vallejo Police Department detectives John Lynch and Ed Rust were assigned to the Ferrin/Mageau case, with detective Jack Mulanax taking over in the 1970s. Napa County sheriff detectives Kenneth Narlow and David Collins were placed in charge of the Shepard/Hartnell case.

The Stine killing drew San Francisco Police Department homicide inspectors David Toschi and William Armstrong into the investigation. They eventually headed up what became known as the Zodiac Squad, which, at its peak, included fifty officers and ten inspectors. "The Z case. . . . That's what we called it," remembers Toschi. "I think Bill [Armstrong] and I might have stepped on some toes because we pushed so hard. But this killer had become the Zodiac Killer. We just wanted to solve it and move on."[48]

Crime Scene Investigation

The starting point for each investigation was the crime scene. Forensic science was not as advanced as it is today, so the importance of finding and retrieving tiny pieces of evidence that the killer might have left behind—a thread, a single strand of hair, or a piece of vegetation—was not fully appreciated. Still, everyone understood that entering or leaving the scene

Several different law enforcement agencies worked on the Zodiac case. The first place each investigation began was at the crime scene.

changed it in some way, and in all cases the areas were protected to prevent evidence from being disturbed or contaminated.

Because the killings were at night, floodlights were usually brought in to illuminate the scenes. Then everything was sketched and photographed for later study. Measurements were taken to record important distances, ranging from how far cars sat off roadways to how far victims had run before being shot down by the killer. Automobiles and the ground immediately adjacent to the attacks were carefully searched in order to find evidence such as bullet casings, footprints, and the like. Lynch stated of the Ferrin/Mageau scene: "We were searching for whatever we could find. . . . They dug a perfect bullet out of the car, one that wasn't smashed."[49]

Items that were judged significant were collected. This ranged from cords used in the Shepard/Hartnell and Edwards/Domingos cases to a man's Timex watch with a broken band, found at the Bates scene. Police bagged and labeled everything and took all the evidence to the lab for later analysis.

A Pattern of Prints

One of the most important parts of the investigation required identifying prints found at the scenes and on letters sent by the killer. The Zodiac boasted that he did not leave fingerprints because he used two coats of airplane cement to cover the ridge and groove patterns on his fingers. Investigators did not believe this was true, however. In the course of the case, they found many fingerprints that were unquestionably left by the killer.

One was found in a phone booth used on September 27, 1969, when the Zodiac made an anonymous call to the Napa Police Department. Investigators quickly traced the call to the phone booth and found a print on the receiver that was still slightly damp from sweat and body oils. Unfortunately, an evidence technician attempted to lift the print before it was dry and ruined it.

Another definitive Zodiac print was found at the Stine crime scene. Wet with blood, it had been left on the door of the cab, and had certainly been made after the shooting. Police lifted it, then, in order to be sure that it was the killer's, they

Investigators were able to find many fingerprints left by the Zodiac killer at his crime scenes and on the letters he sent.

47

Three Types of Prints

There are three basic categories of fingerprints that are routinely collected and accepted as evidence in courts of law. Author N.E. Genge describes these categories as patent, latent, and impressed:

Patent prints sport details easily visible to the naked eye. While this may be true of any print . . . patent generally refers to prints made observable by extra substances which coat the skin and are transferred to some object. At crime scenes, blood may create visible prints. So can oil, ink, catsup, and dozens of other substances. . . .

Latent prints—those not generally visible to the naked eye—result from the transfer of normal oils and salts from the skin to some surface. Like the prints on household appliances, many latent prints pop into view in the right light. Others need augmentation by powder or chemical treatment.

The third type, impressed prints, aren't transfers of any kind but actual physical moldings of a set of friction ridges. Caulk around windows, wax, gum . . . have the potential to contain print impressions. On top of functioning as a natural ink, blood can also become a perfect substance for picking up impression prints as it solidifies.

N.E. Genge, *The Forensic Casebook*, New York: Ballantine, 2002, pp. 28-9.

fingerprinted and eliminated all emergency and law enforcement personnel who might have inadvertently touched the cab. They also checked and eliminated all customers who had ridden in the cab on the day of the murder.

The Zodiac also left fingerprints on his messages. Visible only after the paper had been treated with chemicals such as Ninhydrin and silver nitrate, they were on the letter sent to the Vallejo *Times-Herald* and on the cipher sent to the San Francisco *Examiner* in July 1969. Two prints were lifted from the August 1969 letter. Several were found on an April 28, 1970, letter, and one was found on the letter that arrived after Stine's death.

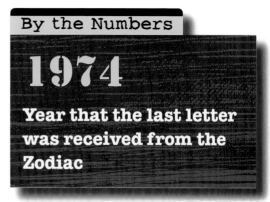

By the Numbers

1974

Year that the last letter was received from the Zodiac

Again, investigators believed that it was unlikely that these prints belonged to someone other than the killer. Because of their incriminating nature, he had likely written and addressed them in secret and then sealed them in envelopes. And, staff at the newspapers were fingerprinted and eliminated.

Moulages and Wing Walkers

Over time, at least thirty-eight fingerprints and three palm prints were sent for analysis and comparison to the FBI's Latent Fingerprint Section of the crime lab in Quantico, Virginia. In addition to fingerprints, shoe and tire prints found at various scenes were analyzed as well.

In the Shepard/Hartnell case, shoe prints were found leading up to Hartnell's car door where the killer had scrawled his message. The prints were photographed, then plaster casts known as moulages were created to preserve them. When measured, they were size 10½ and were deep, indicating that the killer was heavy. "We took a compaction test in the sand," Narlow remembered, "and in order to put that print so deeply in the sand we figured the Zodiac weighed 220 pounds."[50]

Further analysis of the shoe prints revealed a pattern on the sole. This helped investigators identify the footwear as a type of military boot, called a wing walker, manufactured by the International Shoe Company in Philadelphia, Pennsylvania. Wing walkers were not sold in shoe stores, and only a few thousand pairs had been shipped to air force and navy installations on the West Coast. The fact offered a valuable lead. Investigators now believed that the killer was connected to the military in some way.

Tire Prints to Nowhere

Tire prints were also found at the Shepard/Hartnell scene, and technicians photographed them and then cast them in plaster, too. Investigators found that the prints had been made by well-worn tires that were not a matched pair. The distance from the inside of one to the inside of the other was about 52 inches (132cm).

The latter information indicated the killer had been driving a medium-size car, but it did not help investigators link the tires to any particular car. To complicate matters, they knew that the Zodiac had access to at least two cars, because eyewitnesses had described different ones at the scene of different attacks. For instance, a dark, medium-size car with no chrome had been spotted near David Faraday's Rambler the night of the Jensen/Faraday murders. Mike Mageau testified that his attacker

Tire prints found at the Shepard/ Hartnell scene provided some clues to investigators.

had been driving a brown Ford Falcon or Chevrolet Corvair. Kathleen Johns's kidnapper had been driving a light-colored car.

Investigators had to admit that the chances of tracing the Zodiac through tire tracks were slim. Nevertheless, they took down the information and noted various vehicle makes and models that were possible matches. Then they kept their eyes open for a suspect who either owned such cars or was able to borrow them.

By the Numbers

20

Number of hours needed to decipher the first Zodiac cipher

Eyewitness Evidence

At the same time as they analyzed prints, investigators interviewed eyewitnesses to get the best description of the killer. Both Mageau and Hartnell had seen the Zodiac at close range. Both described him as Caucasian, heavy, and dressed in dark clothes. Mageau, who saw him without a mask, gave a statement for a police report: "Subject appeared to be short, possibly 5'8", was real heavy set, beefy build. . . . Subject was not blubbery fat, but real beefy, possibly 195 to 200, or maybe even larger. . . . He had short curly hair, light brown, almost blond. . . . There was nothing unusual about his face, other than that it appeared to be large. . . . The subject did not have a mustache, nor was he wearing glasses or anything. . . . Subject was a white male, approximately 26–30 years."[51]

Other witnesses supported Hartnell's and Mageau's description. A doctor and his sixteen-year-old son and three female sunbathers who were at Lake Berryessa on the afternoon of the Shepard/Hartnell attack reported seeing a man who acted suspiciously. They described him as heavy, with dark hair, a round face, and dark clothes. The sunbathers had seen him more clearly, so police asked them to help create a composite drawing of his face. "This may not be the killer, but we would like to talk with the fellow,"[52] said Don Townsend of the Napa County Sheriff's Office.

Casting Three-Dimensional Impressions

Care and the correct materials are necessary to create accurate copies of tire marks, footprints, or any other impression evidence. Dental stone, a type of plaster used by dentists, is the best choice, because it is harder and resists abrasion better than plaster of paris or modeling plaster. The process of taking an impression is as follows:

1. Place an appropriate amount of water and dental stone in a resealable plastic bag or a bucket and mix for three to five minutes. The material should have the consistency of pancake batter or heavy cream.

2. Carefully preserve the shape and details of the impression by pouring the liquid mixture onto the ground next to it. Allow the liquid to flow into the impression. Fill until the impression overflows with the mixture.

3. While the stone is still impressionable, lightly write the date, collector's initials, and other identifying information onto the cast.

4. Leave the cast undisturbed for twenty to thirty minutes in warm weather, longer in cold weather.

5. Carefully lift the cast out of the impression. Some excavation may be necessary if the impression is made in mud or clay. Allow the cast to air dry for at least forty-eight hours. Package the cast in paper.

The three witnesses to the Stine murder were able to describe the killer, too. The night had been foggy, but they had had an unobstructed view of the cab. They were certain the attacker had been a white male, perhaps in his early forties, with a heavy build, and dark clothes. They judged him to be about 5 feet, 8 inches (1.70m) tall. They also insisted that the man wore glasses, and his short hair appeared reddish brown.

San Francisco patrol officers Donald Fouke and Eric Zelms were on their way to the Stine crime scene when they observed the same man walking down a street. They did not stop or question him because police dispatchers had mistakenly told them to be on the lookout for a black offender. Fouke later described the man as being thirty-five to forty-five years old; about 5 feet, 10 inches (1.75m) tall; 180 to 200 pounds (82 to 91kg), with a medium-heavy build, light-colored short hair, glasses, and dark clothes. Fouke added, "Subject . . . walked with a shuffling lope, slightly bent forward head down."[53]

SAN FRANCISCO POLICE DEPARTMENT

NO. 90-69   WANTED FOR MURDER   OCTOBER 18, 1969

ORIGINAL DRAWING   AMENDED DRAWING

Supplementing our Bulletin 87-69 of October 13, 1969. Additional information has developed the above amended drawing of murder suspect known as "ZODIAC".

WMA, 35-45 Years, approximately 5'8", Heavy Build, Short Brown Hair, possibly with Red Tint, Wears Glasses. Armed with 9 MM Automatic.

Available for comparison: Slugs, Casings, Latents, Handwriting.

ANY INFORMATION:
Inspectors Armstrong & Toschi
Homicide Detail
CASE NO. 696314

THOMAS J. CAHILL
CHIFF OF POLICE

In order to obtain a description of the killer, investigators interviewed several eyewitnesses and were able to come up with a composite sketch of the killer.

Sifting Fact from Fiction

Kathleen Johns's description of her kidnapper differed signifi-
cantly from other eyewitness testimony, leading police to won-
der if she had indeed met the Zodiac. She claimed her abductor
was Caucasian, had brown hair, and wore glasses, but she did
not describe him as heavy. Investigators knew, however, that it
would be easy for the killer to disguise himself by changing his
hair color, donning a pair of glasses, or gaining or losing weight.
They also remembered a phrase from the Zodiac's November 9,
1969, letter that confirmed that possibility. He had written:
"I look like the description passed out only when I do my thing,
the rest of the time I look entirle different."[54]

Even if it was somewhat contradictory, police highly valued
eyewitness testimony. They were more suspicious of random
suggestions from the public, however. "As with any case that
has some notoriety, you have people who want to be detectives and solve the case," says JoAnn West of the Vallejo Police
Department. "Yet they only have a portion of the information;
they don't have the other pieces to the puzzle."[55]

Most of the suggestions proved to be a waste of time. For
instance, one individual thought the police should look for someone named Rush because the phrase "Rush to the Editor" was
on every Zodiac envelope. Others recommended that the police
look for a civil engineer because the symbol the Zodiac used at
the end of his January 29, 1974, letter represented a structural
shape used in building construction. Police checked out most
leads, even if they seemed ridiculous. They remembered Donald
G. Harden's phone call, claiming he had deciphered the first
ciphers. The call had been one of hundreds that had come in, and
it had almost been ignored. No one wanted to be guilty of overlooking a valuable piece of evidence because of carelessness.

Robert Emmet the Hippie

Of the thousands of tips and suggestions that came in over the
years, many had to do with the unsolved ciphers. Even author
Robert Graysmith claimed to have successfully decoded the

Becoming a Questioned Document Examiner

Job Description:
Forensic or questioned document examiners compare questioned handwriting, hand printing, typewriting, commercial printing, photocopies, papers, inks, and other documentary evidence with known samples in order to establish the authenticity of the contested material. Questioned document examiners also serve as expert witnesses in courts of law.

Education:
Aspiring questioned document examiners must complete high school and earn a bachelor's or master's degree from an accredited four-year college or university. They must then serve a minimum of two years apprenticeship in a forensic laboratory recognized by the American Board of Forensic Document Examiners (ABFDE).

Qualifications:
Certification by the ABFDE is recommended.

Additional Information:
Aspiring forensic document examiners must have excellent eyesight. They must also have a great deal of patience as well as the ability to approach a task objectively.

Salary:
$36,000 to $75,000 per year

340-symbol message sent on November 8, 1969. His decoded message made no sense, however, and most did not accept his solution as valid. Of the suggestions having to do with ciphers, many focused on the eighteen letters at the end of the

Author Robert Graysmith attempted to decode one of the ciphers, but his solution was deemed invalid.

first puzzle—*EBEORIETEMETHHPITI.* The Hardens had deciphered them, but they made no sense. Many people believed that, if the letters were transposed, a clue to the Zodiac's name would be revealed. Ideas poured into the police, especially in the days just after the cipher was published.

One person suggested that, when decoded, the letters stood for "San Benito Mental Hospital." This seemed unlikely because no such hospital existed. Another noticed that, if the letters *R*, *M*, and *P* were added and the series rearranged, it spelled out the name Robert Emmet the hippie.

Willing to give the latter suggestion due consideration, police checked out every Robert Emmet they could find. They discovered a statue of Irish patriot Robert Emmet in front of the Academy of Sciences in Golden Gate Park in San Francisco, but no other individual with that name came to light. Then, in 1992, a woman came forward to Vallejo police, stating that she had known a Robert Emmett Rodifer, who had lived in the Vallejo area in the 1960s. He had become a hippie and moved to Germany. Rodifer was located and interviewed, and he stated that he had known one of the Zodiac suspects, Arthur Leigh Allen. The two had been in high school together, and Allen had disliked Rodifer. The association was fascinating, but on its own it was not strong enough evidence for police to arrest Allen.

"I Am Not Avery"

In contrast to the limited assistance the public provided, media cooperation was extremely important to investigators because the killer sent most of his messages to newspapers. Their willingness to turn over letters, publish messages, and/or withhold certain pertinent facts was essential as police struggled to understand and advance the investigation.

One member of the media, *San Francisco Chronicle* reporter Paul Avery, got more than he bargained for when he became involved in the case in 1969. A former war correspondent and licensed private detective, Avery was used to facing danger. Still, after writing a series of articles about the Zodiac, he was startled to receive a Halloween card from the killer. It had a dancing skeleton on the front, and inside the Zodiac had printed the message "Peek-a-boo! You are doomed!"[56]

Avery laughed off the threat, but, at the suggestion of San Francisco police chief Al Nelder, he began carrying a loaded .38-caliber revolver. His colleagues at the *Chronicle* jokingly started wearing lapel buttons that read, "I Am Not Avery," in case the killer should mistake one of them for the journalist. Given the Zodiac's reputation, however, each was aware that the danger could be all too real. *Chronicle* writer Duffy Jennings recalled, "Whenever I left the building with Paul, I couldn't help being more keenly aware of our surroundings. I looked much more carefully around corners, behind us, in parked cars and into the eyes of passing strangers."[57]

Police did not have time to worry about passing strangers in their hunt for the Zodiac. They were too busy probing the lives of hundreds of suspects that came to light during the investigation. They ranged from sailors to salesmen. While each investigator had his or her favorite, nothing definitive ever tied anyone to the crimes. Nevertheless, no one was willing to give up on the case, because many more lives could be at stake.

CHAPTER 4

Strange and Suspicious

Police did not realize that they were looking for a serial kill-er when they began to investigate the first of the Zodiac murders. Thus, they pursued more traditional suspects, such as a troublemaking student named Ricky, who had pestered Betty Lou Jensen for a time at school. After the Ferrin/Mageau attack, they checked out James Phillips, Darlene Ferrin's former husband and "Paul" (not his real name), a bartender who had allegedly been bothering her at work. Griffin R., a patient at Napa State Mental Hospital matched the description of the killer and had been out of the hospital on the weekend of the Shepard/Hartnell attack. Doctors judged that he was capable of committing such violent crimes, but he had not actually done so.

When these men were cleared, they were replaced with others such as "Andrew Walker" (not his real name). Walker received code training while serving in the army air force, had spent considerable time at the restaurant where Ferrin worked, and had been unemployed during the time of known Zodiac activity. Investigators were heartened each time they came across a new suspect, but when no definitive evidence was found to link the suspect to the Zodiac, their hopes for a quick solution to the case faded.

Analyzing the Killer

By 1970 investigators had learned enough about the Zodiac to create a profile—an analysis of the unknown perpetrator's crimes and the way he committed them in order to predict who he was. Profiling was a fairly new profession in 1970, but law enforcement welcomed it as means of helping them solve the case.

Investigators were able to use profiling to analyze the Zodiac killer. Gregg McCrary (pictured) was a former FBI profiler and commented on the case.

Profilers first reviewed the killer's physical description. Witnesses consistently described him as Caucasian, around thirty years old, solidly built, and with short hair. They also noted that he spoke in a monotone voice, devoid of emotion. "Like a . . . student's," remembered Hartnell. "But kind of a drawl; not a Southern drawl, though."[58] Investigators noted that his hair color seemed to change and he sometimes wore glasses as attempts to disguise himself.

They then analyzed the killer's method of operation. He brought along a loaded gun, a knife, and rope to tie up his victims. This indicated that he was organized and capable of thinking, planning, and functioning in society. He probably appeared normal to neighbors and friends. It was possible that he worked during the day, because he only killed in the evening or at night. The fact that cars were always involved in his crimes meant that he had his own means of transportation.

He also had access to a wide variety of weapons. Even the 9-mm shells found at the Ferrin/Mageau and Stine scenes had come from two different weapons. And, all his weapons allowed him to come in contact with his victims. According to Napa County Sheriff's detective Kenneth Narlow, "Certain type assailants use certain weapons because it gets them closer to their victims. If you wanted to go out and kill for the sheer sake of killing you could use a high-powered rifle and a scope and kill at two hundred, three hundred yards. . . . But by plunging a knife into someone it's the most intimate contact you can have with a victim, and there's no question about it, it's where Zodiac gets some of his thrills."[59]

Cruel and Controlling

The fact that the Zodiac conversed with some of his victims before attacking them indicated to profilers that he was a sadist. He got pleasure from watching others suffer. The fact that he went after couples indicated that he was jealous of people in relationships. He did not sexually assault his victims, but he overkilled the women, shooting or stabbing them more times than he did their male companions. To profilers, this indicated strong but confused sexual feelings. Possibly he had a bad relationship with his mother. Possibly he had never had a normal adult relationship with a woman.

The dramatic elements of his crimes—the hooded disguise, the messages, and the codes—highlighted his desire for attention. Taunting the police, leaving false clues, and threatening the public indicated anger and a desire to feel powerful and in control. Former FBI profiler Gregg O. McCrary writes, "He enjoyed the control he exerted because he was in charge; he was running the investigation, more or less, as though he was the supervisor ....When he moved from the Vallejo area into

Taking a Polygraph Test

Polygraph machines, also known as lie detectors, are used to monitor changes that occur in the body during an interview. In the United States, polygraph machines are digitalized instruments with computer monitors. The process of taking a polygraph test is as follows:

1 The subject sits in a chair.

2 The examiner attaches four to six sensors to the subject's body in specific locations to measure breathing rate, pulse, blood pressure, and perspiration.

3 The examiner provides information about the test and instructs the subject to give only "yes" and "no" answers.

4 The examiner starts with a pretest interview of several irrelevant questions to gain preliminary information about subject's normal reaction levels.

5 The examiner administers a stim test, during which subject is asked to deliberately lie. This allows the examiner to understand how the subject reacts to being deceptive.

6 The actual test begins. Some of the questions asked are irrelevant ("Is your name Mary S?"). Some are questions that most people will lie about ("Have you ever stolen money?"). These are called probable-lie questions. The remaining questions are relevant to the topic the examiner is interested in. The different types of questions alternate.

7 The subject passes the test if the measured responses during the probable-lie questions are greater than those elicited during the relevant question portion of the test.

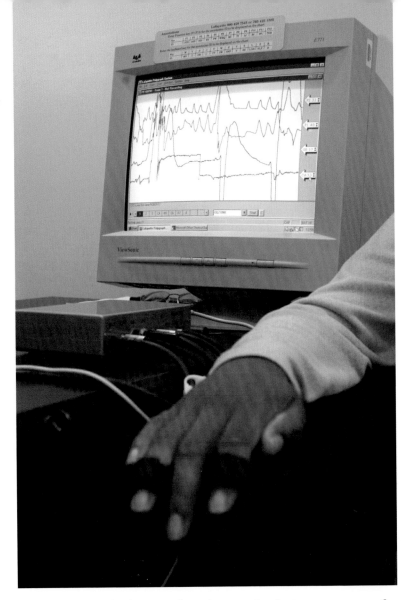

This is an example of a computerized polygraph machine.

San Francisco for his murders, he acquired a greater venue for control, along with the ability to spread the terror and feel more powerful. For him, it was all about that."[60]

His selfishness, deceitfulness, and lack of guilt or remorse about hurting others indicated to profilers that he was a psychopath. Author and psychologist David Van Nuys opined, "It's clear this was a person with an enormous need for attention. He had an immature personality and was clearly filled with rage. He was egotistical, narcissistic [self-absorbed], manipulative. It leads you to the classical psychiatric diagnosis of a psychopathic personality disorder."[61]

Careless or Careful?

The Zodiac was undoubtedly a psychopath, but those who ana-lyzed his crimes disagreed over whether he was calculating and clever, or clumsy and careless. Many opted for the former. They believed he was a brilliant man who was playing a game of hide-and-seek with the police. To back their assertions, they pointed out that he was well educated, as demonstrated by his knowledge of opera, ciphers, bomb making, mathematics, and astrology. All were topics that were not covered in most high school curricula. He had also made a brief reference to "radians" in his July 26, 1970, letter, an unfamiliar term to most people. A radian is an angle of 57.296 degrees, is defined as "an angle subtended by an arc of a circle equal in length to the radius of a circle,"[62] and is commonly used by engineers and mathematicians.

Others insisted that the Zodiac was simply a braggart who made mistakes, lied to try to throw police off his tracks, and avoided capture through sheer luck. He boasted that he did not leave fingerprints, yet police found a number of them on letters and at crime scenes. He threatened to set a bomb, but never carried through with his threat. Bradley J. Fischer, who produced the 2007 movie *Zodiac*, stated, "He's not 'Wile E. Coyote Super Genius,' as we grew fond of calling him, he's a sad, pathetic and incredibly sick person who came within inches of being caught."[63]

Whether intelligent or not, profilers agreed that the Zodiac grew up feeling insecure and unsure of himself. Perhaps he had been abused. Perhaps he had suffered some other traumatic expe-rience. No matter what, he was always trying to prove to himself and others that he was daring and clever. McCrary observes, "The Zodiac needed to think he was smarter than even the best detectives, and [in his mind] he probably exaggerated the risks he took in order to affirm his smug sense of superiority."[64]

Guilty Relatives

With the profile to guide them, police identified and inter-viewed over twenty-five hundred suspects over the years. Promising individuals were always coming to light. "All over the world, people were mesmerized by the Zodiac mystery," stated handwriting expert Lloyd Cunningham, "and everyone's relative or ex-friend became a suspect."[65]

Vallejo attorney William L. Beeman suggested that his brother Jack was the Zodiac. He based his accusations on Jack's grammatical errors, vocabulary, and misspellings that were similar to the killer's. Like the Zodiac, Jack used phrases such as *do my thing* and wrote "buss" instead of "bus" and "takeing" instead of "taking." Jack was also a recluse and hated women. "He said that women were subhumans, that they could not think logically; that they acted on emotion,"[66] Beeman said. Investigators ruled out Jack Beeman after they determined that he was fifty-one years old, did not resemble the Zodiac, and had lung disease so serious that he could not walk without wheezing.

Dennis Kaufman believed his stepfather, Jack Tarrance, was the Zodiac. According to Kaufman, Tarrance was an angry man, who often talked about killing. His appearance and handwriting generally matched the description of the killer. He had been a supply sergeant in the U.S. Air Force, so he

Over 2,500 suspects were interviewed over the years in the Zodiac case. One suspect was accused because his vocabulary, grammatical errors, and misspellings were similar to the killer's.

would have had access to Wing Walker boots. He had been to Japan and the killer's favorite opera, *The Mikado*, was set in Japan. He liked to use a compass and pinpoint exact locations on maps, similar to the way the Zodiac had pinpointed Mount Diablo on a map. Investigators agreed that Tarrance did all those things, but they could not prove that he was the Zodiac. Sonoma County Sheriff Department's Steve Brown stated, "I did some investigation of his [Dennis Kaufman's] father, but I couldn't find anything that said he did it." Former FBI agent Ken Hittmeier observed, "We put Dennis in touch with the SFPD [San Francisco Police Department], but apparently, they were unimpressed."[67]

The Con Artist

Former Sonora police officer Harvey Hines was convinced that ex-convict and con artist Lawrence Kane was the Zodiac. Kane fit the physical description of the killer and was a loner who did not relate well to women. He was secretive, egotistical, and fought with his neighbors. He had once been in the navy, giving him the opportunity to purchase Wing Walker boots.

According to Hines, Darlene Ferrin's sisters had identified Kane's picture as that of a man who had frightened Ferrin in the days before her death. Kane had lived in San Francisco in 1969, just blocks from where Paul Stine was killed. There had also been a theater near his San Francisco residence that was putting on *The Mikado* in 1969. He was living in South Lake Tahoe when Donna Lass disappeared in 1970. Hines also pointed out that Kane had a mental condition that indicated he had "a lack of control in self gratification."[68]

At Hines's urging, police interviewed Kane. They dismissed him as the Zodiac, however, stating that any evidence against him was weak and circumstantial. Hines fumed, "I felt the investigators met with Kane more to shut me up. Kane lied to them repeatedly and they simply took his word for it."[69] Roy Conway of the Vallejo Police Department defended law enforcement's position, however. "Kane is not the Zodiac. I can't tell you how

The Zodiac had made references to a Gilbert and Sullivan light opera known as "The Mikado" in one of his letters and one suspect was interviewed because there was a theater in his neighborhood that was putting on "The Mikado."

much time I've given Harvey [Hines] over the years, but he has nothing of any evidentiary [based on evidence] value. We can't make a case with it, let alone get a conviction."[70]

The Theater Manager

Police could not make a case against radio engineer and theater manager Richard Reed Marshall, either. Considered a good suspect for a time, the stocky, bespectacled Marshall conformed loosely to eyewitness descriptions of the Zodiac. Circumstantial evidence linked him to the case, too. He had been in the navy, had been trained in codes, and knew how to sew. The latter skill would have been used in constructing the hooded disguise the Zodiac wore during the Shepard/Hartnell attack.

Marshall had owned a home in Riverside, California, at the time of Cheri Jo Bates's murder. Allegedly he had lived just a few blocks from Ferrin when she was married to her first husband. He owned a portable Royal typewriter, similar to the one used to type one of the Riverside letters. His print-ing was similar to that found in the Zodiac letters, and, like the Zodiac, he was a Gilbert and Sullivan fan. Investigators also learned that he owned a copy of *El Spectre Rojo* (The Red Phantom), a rare silent movie. If he were the Zodiac, that movie might have prompted him to sign the July 1974 letter as The Red Phantom.

Despite all the circumstantial evidence, profilers pointed out that Marshall's personality did not fit the Zodiac profile. Specifically, he was not known to be controlling or violent. And there was nothing factual such as a fingerprint to link him to the killings. Napa County detective Narlow remained suspicious of Marshall but admitted, "We've all got our favor-ites. [Detectives David] Toschi and [William] Armstrong were always high on [Arthur Leigh Allen]. I've been high on [Marshall]. We're all just guessing."[71]

The Teacher

Among all the favorites, Arthur Leigh Allen was the most pop-ular suspect in the Zodiac case. In fact, many people were so convinced he was the Zodiac that not even scientific evidence could change their minds. Police served three search warrants on Allen over the years—on September 14, 1972; February 14, 1991; and August 28, 1992. Nevertheless, all of the allegations against him were based on circumstantial evidence and police could never definitively connect him to the killings.

Allen was a Vallejo resident, who lived with his mother until her death in 1989. Caucasian, about 6 feet (1.8m) tall, and 240 pounds (109kg), he fit the physical description of the killer. He had worked as a sailmaker at Mare Island Naval Shipyard in Vallejo, and he had been in the navy. He had been an elementary school teacher in the 1960s, but had been fired for having a loaded weapon in his car on school grounds. He had also been fired from a second teaching job for molesting a student. Members of his family stated that he hated women and had never had a serious relationship with one. He had been

Suspicious Property

Investigators searched suspect Arthur Leigh Allen's home in 1991 and found a variety of suspicious items. Some are listed below. A complete list is available on www.zodiackiller.com/AllenWarrant.html.

1 Four pipe bombs

2 Two safety fuses

3 Nine blasting caps

4 Two 1-inch (2.5cm) galvanized pipes with one end cap

5 One cardboard box with fireworks, safety fuses, bottles of potassium nitrate

6 One can of black powder

7 Ruger .22 revolver and six live rounds of ammunition

8 Ruger .44 Blackhawk revolver and five rounds of ammunition

9 Colt .32 auto pistol and seven rounds of ammunition

10 Winchester, Super, and miscellaneous ammunition

11 Zodiac Sea Wolf watch

12 Miscellaneous papers and news clippings

13 Marlin .22 rifle with scope

14 Inland .30 caliber rifle

15 Royal manual typewriter

16 Small flashlight

17 Hunting knife with sheath and rivets

18 Remington .22 short caliber rifle

19 Stevens Model B35 twelve-gauge double-barrel shotgun

20 Winchester Model 50 twenty-gauge automatic shotgun

interviewed by Vallejo Police Department detective John Lynch in October 1969 after the Shepard murder, but had never been considered a suspect.

In 1971 a former acquaintance of Allen came forward with a story that caused police to seriously consider him a suspect. Donald Cheney stated that he had been on a hunting trip with Allen in early 1969. One night around the campfire, Allen had talked about wanting to hunt people using a flashlight attached to a gun. He had talked about shooting children and had said that if he became a killer, he would distract and confuse authorities by sending them letters, which he would sign "Zodiac." Police liked what they heard, but paused when they discovered that Allen had allegedly made inappropriate advances toward Cheney's young daughter. This might have given Cheney a motive to make a false accusation about his former friend.

Disappointment

When another individual supported Cheney's allegation that Allen was fascinated with hunting people, the need to investigate him was clear. Thus, on August 4, 1971, detectives Toschi, Armstrong, and Jack Mulanax set up an interview at Union Oil, where Allen worked as a junior chemist. During that interview, Allen was pleasant and claimed he had not

been following the Zodiac case and did not know much about it. He then freely volunteered information that seemed to contradict that claim. He stated that he had lived in Southern California at the approximate time of the Bates murder; and that he had had bloody knives in his car (allegedly used to kill chickens) on the day police had interviewed him in 1969. He revealed that he had read "The Most Dangerous Game" in high school and that it had made a lasting impression on him. He showed police the Zodiac brand watch he wore and explained that it had been a Christmas gift from his mother in 1967 or 1968. Police noted that the crossed-circle symbol used by the Zodiac killer was on the face of the watch.

Allen was the best suspect they had found thus far, but Toschi and Armstrong knew that they still needed physical evidence to arrest him. In an attempt to get that evidence, they asked Allen's brother, Ron to search the basement where Allen lived in his mother's house. Serial killers are known to keep souvenirs or trophies of their crimes in order to relive the incident. Ron was to specifically look for the hooded disguise, knives, Stine's missing keys, and pieces of Stine's bloody shirt. Ron stated that he doubted that his brother could be a serious suspect in the case, but agreed to cooperate. During his search, he found some general material having to do with ciphers, but nothing specific to the Zodiac.

By September 1972, investigators were still interested in Allen and judged they had probable cause to apply for a warrant to search a trailer he owned in Santa Rosa,

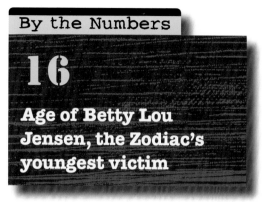

By the Numbers

16

Age of Betty Lou Jensen, the Zodiac's youngest victim

California. Santa Rosa is 25 miles (40km) from Napa. They reasoned that Allen might have hidden incriminating evidence someplace away from his home. A Sonoma County judge granted the warrant, and police entered the trailer while Allen was away. It was littered with papers and trash, and the bodies of several dissected squirrels were found stored in the freezer. The latter appeared suspicious because psychopaths often take pleasure in torturing animals. Nevertheless, no Zodiac material was found, and when Allen returned to the trailer, he explained that he was earning a degree in biology at Sonoma State College and had obtained permission to experiment on the animals. Investigators fingerprinted him, collected a sample of his handwriting (right and left hands), and requested that he take a polygraph test. He passed the polygraph, and comparisons of his prints to those on Stine's cab did not match. His handwriting was not consistent with writing in the Zodiac messages either.

New Allegations

The disappointing findings convinced most investigators that Allen was not the Zodiac. Others were unwilling to dismiss him, however. They suggested that fingerprints might have belonged to a police officer or someone else who had somehow contaminated the scene. They speculated that Allen might have had an accomplice who wrote letters and left fingerprints

Setback

Investigation of Arthur Leigh Allen suffered a serious setback on August 26, 1992, when fire and ambulance personnel found his lifeless body in his basement apartment. He had died of kidney failure, a complication of diabetes.

Police obtained a search warrant and seized a relatively new computer Allen owned, as well as some videotapes that were labeled "Z." Nothing contained evidence that indicated Allen was the Zodiac. Nevertheless, some investigators believed they had found their killer, and that, given enough time, they would have brought him to justice. "I believe as I always have the Zodiac was Arthur Leigh Allen," [Vallejo police officer Roy] Conway stated in 1994. "If Allen were alive today, we would file charges against him as the Zodiac."

Quoted in Rider McDowell, "On the Trail of the Zodiac," May 8–15, 1994. http://www.zodiackiller.com/KH15.html

on the paper. They insisted that he might have disguised his writing in some way to deceive everyone.

While suspicions continued, Allen was convicted of child molestation in 1974 and incarcerated in Atascadero State Hospital, a maximum-security psychiatric facility. Coincidently, the Zodiac letters also ended at that time. Allen was released in the summer of 1977. He returned to his family home and drifted from job to job.

In 1990 investigators' interest in Allen was again revived when convicted armed robber Ralph Spinelli came forward with a new allegation. Spinelli was a former friend of Allen's and claimed that the day before Stine's murder, Allen had told him he was going to San Francisco and kill a cab driver. The allegation reopened the case for review, and police noted that they had never searched Allen's Vallejo home or a 22-foot (7m) sailboat that he kept stored at a friend's home. After obtaining a warrant, they did so in February 1991.

"I Am Not the Zodiac"

The search of Allen's boat revealed nothing, but his basement apartment contained a great deal of suspicious material. Police uncovered sadistic pornographic videos, a large knife, a small flashlight, and news clippings relating to the Zodiac case. There was also a cache of weapons and bomb-making supplies, items that Allen was not allowed to possess because he was a convicted felon. Police confiscated everything from the Zodiac watch to two typewriters. They found nothing that absolutely identified Allen as the Zodiac, however, and therefore did not arrest him.

With police activity around the Allen home, word leaked to neighbors and then the public that he was a Zodiac suspect. He tried to counter suspicions by allowing himself to be interviewed by newspaper and television reporters and continually protested his innocence. "They haven't arrested me because they can't prove a thing," he told one interviewer. "The only way I can clear myself would be for the real Zodiac to confess, if he's still alive. I am not the Zodiac. I've never killed anyone."[72]

While the media pursued Allen, investigators sat back and tried to determine what to do next. They had no conclusive physical evidence against anyone. They had no one else to investigate. They did not want to quit, but after twenty years, all were discouraged and disillusioned. "This is a very frustrating case," said Narlow. "You try not to let it become personal, but after so many years it does take a toll because it's so challenging."[73]

Going Nowhere

Frustration was a hallmark of the Zodiac case almost from the beginning. Investigators not only pursued a cunning killer, but they also struggled with inexperience, questionable evidence, copycats, and amateur sleuths, who created confusion and controversy. "Everyone was going different ways with all kinds of leads," Benecia police officer Pierre Bidou said. "We had a sketch, look-alikes and different sightings."[74]

Slow Start

Much early confusion stemmed from the fact that, in the 1960s, few law enforcement officials were familiar with the concept of "stranger murders." Serial killers, people who mur-

Serial killers (like Gary Ridgway pictured here) were rare during the time of the Zodiac killings. As a result, progress and time were lost as investigators tried to focus and connect the killings.

dered for pleasure and attacked perfect strangers, were rare in that era. Valuable time was lost before detectives changed focus and realized that they were chasing a man who enjoyed killing for its own sake, who put a great deal of planning into his murders, and who chose his victims for symbolic reasons.

Even after serial killing was better understood, the fact that the murders took place in different counties and police jurisdictions hampered progress. Files were not easily accessible, and information was not always freely shared. Territorial feelings meant that officers who investigated in neighboring jurisdictions had to be careful not to infringe upon their fellow colleagues' work. Some investigators held back their hunches and theories because each department wanted to be the first to solve a case. Former Vallejo police officer Tony Pearsall observed, "You didn't get a lot of cooperation between agencies. Investigators I talked to were continually frustrated over it, because they never knew if all the agencies were sharing everything with everybody."[75]

In an effort to counter those obstacles, a Zodiac seminar was held in San Francisco on October 20, 1969. Investigators from precincts where the Zodiac had killed were invited to attend, as were BCII experts, U.S. postal inspectors, FBI representatives, and members of Naval Intelligence. The effort helped, but did not eliminate all barriers.

Which Victims?

Uncertainty over who was and was not a Zodiac victim created additional obstacles to solving the case. Most Bay Area police, for instance, were convinced that the Zodiac killed Cheri Jo Bates. Riverside police, however, believed she was killed by a local man, as detective Steven Shumway emphasized to Zodiac enthusiast Tom Voigt in 2003: "There are two things for sure you can share with your many readers: There was a murderer who called himself the Zodiac and there was the murderer who killed Cheri. They are two different people."[76] With that mindset, Riverside did not pursue the Zodiac link as zealously as other investigators did.

The same was true with the Donna Lass case. Based on handwriting expert Sherman Morrill's conclusions, some believed she was a Zodiac victim. Others could not wholeheartedly support that theory. They pointed out that the MO did not fit the Zodiac, and there was no other evidence to support the theory. South Lake Tahoe police chief Ray Lauritzen expressed his skepticism when he stated, "I suppose the Zodiac theory is as good as any. We most certainly are checking into this possibility because of the postcard sent to the *Chronicle*."[77]

On the Wrong Track

The police's tendency to go after traditional suspects with traditional motives slowed the initial Zodiac investigation. In Tom Voigt's article, "The Lake Herman Tragedy" on Zodiackiller.com, Shannon, a friend of Betty Lou Jensen, recalls their treatment of her and her friends at the time.

I was sitting across the desk from [Detective Les] Lundblad. [Detective Russ] Butterbach turned my chair to face him and he pushed his chair up to mine so my knees were touching his and he was leaning over yelling about how this was a killing about drugs and they went to a drug party out there on Lake Herman Road. I kept telling them no, Betty Lou didn't do drugs and neither did David. But they could never get past that; they were sure it was drug-related.

They had me looking at mug shots and cars from a book because they had some idea about a white car or something. They wanted me and my friends to tell them who did drugs in the school and who sold drugs in the school. And if we didn't, they would tell my parents that I did drugs. They had us all scared to death. After we went back to school, they kept calling me and threatening to tell my parents we were doing drugs. The cops followed us. They would follow us at school. They would be on the school grounds and followed us for a week or so whenever we went to the store or someplace else.

Tom Voigt, "The Lake Herman Tragedy," Zodiackiller.com, December 20, 2003.
www.zodiackiller.com/LHR2.html.

The inability to confirm or eliminate victims handicapped the investigators. Without knowing for sure which victims were killed by the Zodiac, they could not know when the killings started and if and when they stopped. They did not know if they should widen their investigation to include cases like the Edwards/Domingos murders in Santa Barbara County or not. If additional murders were Zodiac killings and were not investigated, valuable evidence might never be recovered. If they were not Zodiac killings, investigators would be wasting time and resources that could better be used elsewhere.

Copycat Writers

Besides debate over victims, questions about the authenticity of certain Zodiac letters confused the investigation. Each message thought to come from the killer had to be studied, authenticated, or dismissed, and the process was sometimes so difficult that even the top experts disagreed.

Early messages, which contained information only the killer would know as well as pieces of Paul Stine's bloody shirt, were relatively easy to judge. Later letters were usually compared to these, but as years passed, the Zodiac style changed somewhat. For instance, his lettering went from having a definite right-hand slant, to being straight up and down. And the lettering in the "Red Phantom" letter of July 1974 had long dramatic tails that—to an amateur—looked entirely different from earlier printing.

Copycat writers added to the confusion. Police regularly received notes and letters that contained threats and wild claims. Usually the fakes were relatively easy to spot. The handwriting was dramatically different or the sender had cut and pasted his words together from newspapers and magazines. Some fakes were so good, however, that it took time and a skilled examiner to make a determination.

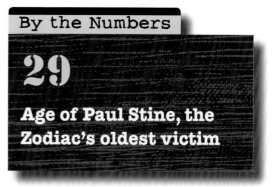

By the Numbers

29

Age of Paul Stine, the Zodiac's oldest victim

"There's a rhythm in writing," explained Lloyd Cunningham, who studied the Zodiac letters for years and felt confident he could detect forgeries. "If someone tries to copy or disguise their handwriting, it's no longer spontaneous."[78]

"That City Pig Toschi"

Despite experts' skill and confidence, debate over the authenticity of one letter became so heated in 1974 that it temporarily sidetracked the investigation and almost ruined the reputation of San Francisco detective David Toschi. The letter arrived on April 24, and read:

> Dear Editor:
> This is the Zodiac speaking I am back with you. Tell [columnist] herb caen I am here, I have always been here. That city pig toschi is good. But I am smarter and better he will get tired then leave me alone. I am waiting for a good movie about me. who will play me. I am now in control of all things. Yours truly: [crossed-circle]—guess SFPD—O."[79]

Within hours, U.S. postal expert John Shimoda authenticated the letter. However, on June 6, problems arose. *Chronicle* columnist Armistead Maupin reported that the tone of the letter was similar to some anonymous fan letters he had received two years previously. At that time, Maupin had created a fictional detective serial called Tales of the City for the *Chronicle*, and it had featured Toschi catching a Zodiac-like killer in the final episode. Shortly thereafter, the fan letters arrived, praising both the serial and the detective. Maupin had suspected that Toschi himself had written them, and now—because of the similarities and the fact that Toschi had been mentioned by name—he suspected that the detective had written the Zodiac letter, too.

Confronted with the accusation, Toschi confessed to writing the fan letters. "It was a very foolish thing to do. I am

"It's Never Left Me"

Hunting the Zodiac became San Francisco detective David Toschi's life's work, and he found he could never leave the case behind. A 2007 article titled "Detective Hopes Zodiac Film Prompts New Lead in Case," states, "Every year at 9:59 P.M. on Oct. 11 Dave Toschi drives to the Presidio Heights intersection in San Francisco, parks his car, watches and waits. It is a ritual he has performed for 36 years." Toschi explains:

> I make it a point to cross that intersection all the time, especially every anniversary. A lot of times I go and stop and think about it, the prints and the blood. I just stop to see if maybe somebody else would be parked there, maybe the killer would show up. I was always trying to figure out where did we go wrong? It's never left me.

PR-Inside.com, "Detective Hopes Zodiac Film Prompts New Lead in Case," PR-Inside.com, February 28, 2007. www.pr-inside.com/entertainment-blog/2007/02/28/ detective-hopes-zodiac-film-prompts-new.

ashamed of it," he said. He insisted, however, that he had not faked a Zodiac letter. "I wrote no Zodiac letter. I don't need another letter. It only brings me tons of extra work."[80]

Tarnished Reputation

Toschi's superiors were unconvinced by his protests, primarily because Shimoda changed his view about the letter. He and three other questioned documents experts—Robert Prouty and Terrence Pascoe of the BCII, and Keith Woodward, former chief of the Los Angeles Police Department's Questioned Document Department—studied it in-depth and decided that it was a fake. They believed it had been carefully created by someone who had seen authentic letters and had been able to copy them. Prouty stated, "My first impression was that it was in the same general style as previous letters, but after closer examination my ultimate conclusion was that there were so many differences that it was not written by the same person who wrote the previous Zodiac letters."[81]

Handwriting expert Morrill disagreed with the others. Staunchly loyal to Toschi, he declared, "This last letter that turned up is definitely by the Zodiac we knew in the past. I examined it. The characters and handwriting are just dead-bang the same."[82]

Toschi was never formally accused, but after a departmental internal affairs investigation, his superiors moved him from homicide to pawnshop detail. He continued to declare his innocence, and the experts continued to debate the letter's authenticity. He was allowed to return to homicide a year later, but his reputation was irreparably tarnished. Controversy over the letter remains.

Amateur Sleuths

At the time of Toschi's reassignment, he was the only San Francisco detective left working on the Zodiac case. With the passing of months and years, law enforcement had exhausted all its leads. Tips came in regularly—about one per week—but most stemmed from psychics, cranks, or people who were angry with a neighbor or coworker. Letters from people claiming to be the Zodiac had grown fewer, too. Eventually, police focused on more current issues, detectives were assigned to other projects, and everyone forgot the killer, except for a number of amateur sleuths.

Amateur sleuths would not let the case die. They were intent on learning all they could, and they grew in number

Personal computers increased in popularity during the 1980s and 1990s. Web sites devoted to the Zodiac case were created and amateurs were able to immerse themselves in the case.

as time passed. One of them, filmmaker John Mikulenka, explained their continuing interest: "I think it's a real need for and appreciation for mystery. It's a mental exercise too, trying to figure out the different angles, trying to bring more light to a cold case."[83]

As personal computers developed in the 1980s and 1990s, the amateurs were able to immerse themselves in the case. Several Web sites devoted to the Zodiac were created. They included biographies of victims and suspects, photos of crime scenes, police reports, and message boards where everything from ciphers to Satanism could be discussed. Enthusiasts became known as Zodiologists, Zodiofiles, or Zodiobuffs, and some were not content to merely chat online. Instead, they gathered annually at one of the crime scenes to see everything firsthand and look for leads. Participants traveled from as far away as Hawaii, and ranged from doctors to pilots to victim Darlene Ferrin's brother Leo Suennen. "Most people attracted to this case are very cerebral, creative and intelligent," Voigt observes. "Granted, some are also very unusual. I'm hoping that gathering them in one spot to share ideas and theories will produce information that might help advance the case."[84]

Amateur Theories

Most Zodiobuffs were convinced that the police had somehow overlooked some vital detail that would identify the killer, and they poured over the evidence tirelessly. As a result, theories about the case multiplied. Some believed the Zodiac was a police officer or a newsman who had worked at one of the San Francisco papers. Some believed there might have been cooperation between several suspects, such as Allen and Kane. Some were convinced the killings were linked to witchcraft or phases of the moon.

A few theorized that the Zodiac was one of several notorious killers who had once lived in the Bay Area. They pointed

Some individuals believed that the Zodiac was Unabomber Ted Kaczynski who had lived in the Bay Area.

New Evidence?

In March 2007 Zodiac enthusiast Tom Voigt was excited to learn that a 1990 Christmas card, misplaced in San Francisco Chronicle files, might have been sent by the Zodiac. Handwriting expert Lloyd Cunningham dismissed the letter as an imitation, but Voigt was not convinced as Rich Freedman relates in the following excerpt from a newspaper article:

Tom Voigt, the man admittedly obsessed with Zodiac since childhood and Webmaster of zodiackiller.com, firmly believes a recently found 1990 Christmas card postmarked from Eureka is authentic.

"I've been told it is without a doubt, Zodiac," Voigt said. . . . "If it's a fake, it's the greatest fake I've ever seen.". . .

The card was a "secret pal" style that Zodiac had sent to the *Chronicle* during his killing spree in 1968 and '69. Inside the card was a carpenter's pencil and U.S. postal keys, "which could be a clue to who the Zodiac was," said Voigt, who was forwarded scans of the card. . . .

The card and envelope are in the hands of the Vallejo Police Department and "if there's any potential that [it] would yield a new finding, we will submit it" to a DNA examiner, said Lt. Rick Nichelman. . . . Nichelman said the public should understand the dilemma of working with 17-year-old alleged evidence in a 40-year-old case. "But if something is unturned, who knows?"

Rich Freedman, "Zodiac: Did Killer Send Card in 1990?" *Times-Herald*, March 4, 2007.

out that Unabomber Ted Kaczynski had been a professor at the University of California at Berkeley in 1969. He had set bombs and written taunting letters to the press. There was also Bruce

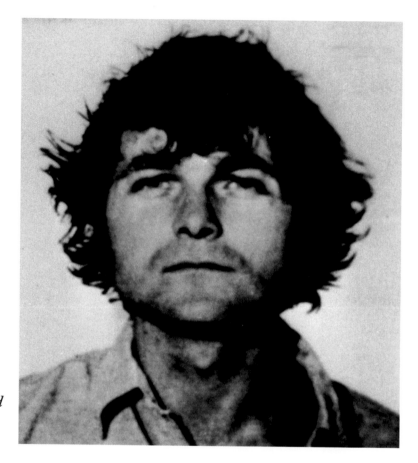

Others believed that Bruce Davis, who helped the Manson family commit murders, could have been the Zodiac killer because, he too, had lived in the Bay Area in the 1960s.

Davis, known for participating in serial murders carried out by the infamous Manson family. He had lived in the Bay Area in the late 1960s as well. Thinking along the same lines, the FBI and the BCII checked both men, but found no evidence linking them to the attacks. Imprisoned for other crimes, they were conclusively cleared of the Zodiac murders.

Some enthusiasts were so excited about their theories that they went to the police with them. One group demanded the investigation of their favorite suspect, Robert E. Hunter Jr., a wealthy San Francisco banker who had allegedly lived in the neighborhood where Stine was killed. They reminded police of the desktop poem found in Riverside, which had been signed "rh." Those were Hunter's initials. When police checked on Hunter, however, they discovered that he had moved into the neighborhood where Stine was killed after the murder. They also could find no proof that Hunter wrote the desktop poem. Apparently only faulty reasoning and coincidence connected the banker to the Zodiac crimes.

Obsessions

A few individuals became so obsessed with the case that they were unable to think of anything else. Former *Chronicle* political-cartoonist-turned-author Robert Graysmith was one such individual. He said of the first Zodiac letter he saw: "I looked at the small printing on the letter. . . . Primarily, I felt rage at the coldness, arrogance and insanity of the murderer. . . . [But] the letter's strangeness ensnared me. Irretrievably hooked, immediately obsessed, I wanted to solve what I felt was to become one of the great mysteries."[85]

Robert Graysmith became obsessed with the Zodiac case and wrote several books about it.

Tom Voigt became obsessed with the Zodiac case after hearing about it on the television show Unsolved Mysteries *in 1995. (Shown here is a scene from the show.)*

Graysmith spent years poring over Zodiac documents and interviewing survivors and investigators. In the process, he became convinced that former teacher Allen was the Zodiac, and even went so far as to shadow the man at home and at work. Graysmith's personal investigation continued until he had gathered more than a ton of material that filled boxes from floor to ceiling in his apartment. Eventually he used that material to write two books about the Zodiac. In the process, however, other aspects of his life suffered. "I lost a lot of weight, my marriage broke up, I got fairly sick . . . I wrote . . . because I had to," he said. "I got totally involved in it."[86]

Commercial Web designer Tom Voigt is another who became obsessed with the Zodiac. His fascination began when the case was featured on the TV show *Unsolved Mysteries* in 1995.

After spending several years and thousands of dollars in research, Voigt started a Zodiac Web site in March 1998. The site eventually expanded to six thousand pages, and Voigt became known as one of the top Zodiac experts in the world. "The fact is," he says, "this guy turned himself into a super-villain through his own doing. He was like a villain out of the Batman comics. He gave himself his own nickname, he taunted not only the police but the public, sending letters that included physical evidence. Just his handwriting was evidence, and he knew it. He would say, 'Here is everything you need to catch me, and I'll bet you still can't do it.' And guess what: He was right."[87]

Penn's Radian Theory

One of the most unconventional individuals to become obsessed with the Zodiac case was author and cipher analyst Gareth Penn. Penn developed what became known as the Radian Theory based on the Zodiac letter that included a map of the Bay Area with Mount Diablo marked with the crossed-circle symbol and a postscript that explained, "The Mt. Diablo code concerns radians, + # inches along the radians."[88]

Penn explained his Radian Theory in his essay, "Times 17: The Amazing Story of the Zodiac Murders in California and Massachusetts, 1966–1981." In it, he theorized that the killer was murdering to create a giant figure on the landscape and had chosen his victims based on their location rather than their identity. Author Curt Rowlett explains, "Gareth Penn has theorized that cabdriver Stine may have been chosen because Zodiac needed a victim whom he could place in a certain area at a certain time; all in order to complete the premeditated construction of a huge, connect-the-dots-to-the-murder-sites, geometric shape over the San Francisco Bay Area."[89]

Penn's Radian Theory was considered credible by some, but his announcement that he had identified the Zodiac in 1981 was not. His suspect was University of California, Berkeley professor Michael O'Hare, and Penn announced that he had determined O'Hare was the Zodiac through the use of Morse

Gareth Penn was an author and cipher analyst who developed the Radian Theory on the Zodiac killer. He believed that Michael O'Hare, a professor at the University of California, Berkeley (pictured here) was the killer. His theory wasn't considered credible.

code and binary mathematics. The accusation made national headlines but was not taken seriously because O'Hare was a well-respected professional, and there was no evidence against him. Voigt opined, "There is simply nothing solid to implicate Michael O'Hare in the Zodiac crimes. In fact, it is the opinion of more than one researcher that Penn himself makes a much better candidate to be the Zodiac than does O'Hare."[90]

Many people scoffed at Penn and other Zodiac enthusiasts, pointing out that it was unlikely that they could solve a case that had baffled experts for decades. Others, however, insisted that their quest should not be downplayed or discounted. They might never identify the Zodiac, but they could keep the case from being forgotten. Their interest could also motivate law enforcement to continue to look for the killer. Author Michael D. Kelleher emphasized, "Their role really shouldn't be to solve the case. It should be to keep it in the public eye. That's a very important part of solving a cold case."[91]

CHAPTER 6

Beyond the Zodiac Murders

With the Zodiac case now cold, those who had been involved in it in the 1970s and 1980s had to move on. William Armstrong, Kenneth Narlow, John Lynch, Ed Rust, Sherman Morrill, and Lloyd Cunningham retired. David Toschi left the force and became a private detective. Paul Avery died in December 2000. Toschi remembers, "At the end Paul was doing cocaine and he was on a [portable oxygen] machine. He was in really bad shape."[92]

Surviving Zodiac victim Michael Mageau, permanently scarred by his encounter with the killer, lived the life of a drifter. Bryan Hartnell became an attorney in Southern California. He refused to let the incident scar him. "I'm not a victim. I'm not defined by this. The minute you let that be the defining point, then he's in control of my life—not me."[93]

Zodiac Entertainment

As the case slipped from the headlines, it became a lasting part of American culture. The entertainment industry repeatedly drew on the Zodiac for inspiration. The 1971 Clint Eastwood movie *Dirty Harry* featured a character named Scorpio, who wrote letters to the *San Francisco Chronicle* and terrorized the Bay Area. The movie *The Zodiac Killer* was released in 1971. *The Limbic Region*, based on the Zodiac case and starring Edward James Olmos, came out in 1996. *Zodiac Killer* and *The Zodiac* were released in 2005. In 2007 David Fincher's Hollywood thriller *Zodiac*, based on Robert Graysmith's books *Zodiac* and *Zodiac Unmasked*, attracted large audiences and made over $33 million at the box office.

Television crime dramas also incorporated aspects of the Zodiac case into their plots. For instance, in the 1970s series *Hawaii Five-O*, an unscrupulous reporter exploited the crimes of a Zodiac-like killer. *Nash Bridges* produced an episode about the Zodiac in 1996. The series *Millenium* alluded to the Zodiac in the 1998 episode "The Mikado."

In 2007, David Fincher released the thriller Zodiac, *starring Jake Gyllenhaal and Robert Downey, Jr., left.*

A number of novels were written about or inspired by the Zodiac. These include Jerry Weissman's *The Zodiac Killer*, published in 1979, the 1983 work *Legion* by William Peter Blatty, and David Baldacci's 2004 novel *Hour Game*. Then there were various music groups beginning with The Zodiac, formed in the late 1960s. The heavy metal group Macabre included a song titled "Zodiac" on their 1993 *Sinister Slaughter* album. The lyrics of the song were based on the Zodiac letters. The group Machine Head included the song "Blood of the Zodiac" on their 1997 *The More Things Change* album. The Zodiac Killers, a San Francisco punk band, released their first album *The Most Thrilling Experience* in 1999.

Childhood Fears

David Fincher was seven years old and living in the Bay Area when the Zodiac was active in 1969. Fincher would later direct the 2007 movie Zodiac. *In a review on the JIVE Magazine* Web site, *Fincher remembers how, as a child, he walked in fear of the unseen killer.*

If you grew up here, at that time, you had this childhood fear that you kind of insinuated yourself into it. What if it was our bus? What if he showed up in our neighborhood? You create even more drama about it when you're a kid because that is what kids do. I grew up in Marin [County] and now I know about the geography of where the crimes took place, but when you're in grade school, children don't think about that. They think 'He's going to show up at our school.'

JIVE Magazine, Zodiac movie review, *JIVE Magazine,* March 1, 2007. www.jivemagazine.com/review.php?rid=2247.

New York Zodiac

The case not only inspired artists, but it also influenced at least two copycat serial killers. In 1989 New York police began receiving letters that opened with the greeting "This is the Zodiac." In mostly nonsensical ramblings, the writer of the letters announced that a series of murders would take place in the coming months. There would be one murder for each sign of the Zodiac. Each letter was signed with an inverted cross, topped by three number sevens. Because of the differences in content and style, police did not believe that this Zodiac was the same man who had killed in San Francisco twenty years before.

The Zodiac case inspired a copycat serial killer in New York.

The murders occurred as announced, but this time police were able to catch the killer. On June 18, 1996, twenty-nine-year-old Heriberto "Eddie" Seda held three people hostage after having an argument with his sister. Finally taken into custody, Seda wrote out a confession at the police station and signed it with the Zodiac's symbol. One officer immediately recognized it. "It just jumped out of the page," said detective Joseph Herbert. "I nearly fell off my chair."[94]

In 1998 Seda was convicted of murdering three people and wounding four during his six-year killing spree. He was sentenced to more than 150 years in prison.

Kobe Zodiac

In 1997 police in Japan discovered that the Zodiac had inspired a copycat in their country, too. On May 24 of that year, eleven-year-old Jun Hase was killed. Police found a note stuffed in Hase's mouth that read in part: "This is the beginning of the game. . . . You police guys stop me if you can. . . .

Unsolved Mystery

Unlike many other serial murderers, the Zodiac managed to keep his identity a mystery. In an article titled "The Zodiac Machine," author Michael Butterfield points out that other aspects of case remain a mystery, too.

Theories and attempts to explain the Zodiac crimes are tempting, but the Zodiac's motives remain just as much a mystery as his identity. His writings remain inexplicably strange in the annals of crime. His desire to spread fear is well known, and his delight in teasing the world with clues to his identity is surpassed only by his ability to keep his identity a secret. Zodiac fed both the public's fear of violence and its desire for sensational exploitation of tragedy. Zodiac made fear profitable. He was not the first and he most certainly was not the last.

Michael P. Butterfield, "The Zodiac Machine," Jake Wark's "This is the Zodiac Speaking . . ." Web site, 2006. http://members.aol.com/Jakewark/zmachine.html.

I desperately want to see people die, it is a thrill for me to commit murder."[95] A crosslike symbol was inscribed at the end of the message.

In the next few weeks, newspapers in Kobe received several more letters, similar in tone to the one found on Hase. Police vigorously investigated the killing, and on June 28, arrested fourteen-year-old middle school student "Seito Sakakibara" (not his real name). Sakakibara soon confessed to having killed Hase. He also confessed to killing ten-year-old Ayaka Yamashita in March 1997 and to attacking three other schoolgirls in February and March of that year. The style of Sakakibara's killings, along with his notes, was strongly reminiscent of the Zodiac. Friends testified that he had been fascinated with Robert Graysmith's book *Zodiac* when it was published in Japan.

By the Numbers

18.5

Number of murders that occurred per 100,000 people in San Francisco by the late 1970s

At the time of the murders, a minor could not be charged as an adult in Japan, so Sakakibara was sent to a youth reformatory for treatment. In 2004 at the age of twenty-one, he was declared cured of his compulsion to kill and released on parole. His parole ended on December 31, 2004, and he immediately disappeared. In 2000 the Japanese government lowered the age of criminal responsibility from sixteen to fourteen as a result of the Sakakibara murders.

The Final Disappointment

By the year 2000, scientific developments had reached a stage where Bay Area investigators had a new weapon to use in the hunt for the Zodiac. Genetic fingerprinting, the practice of identifying individuals using samples of their deoxyribonucleic acid (DNA), allowed scientists to match suspects to crimes as well as eliminate them when their DNA did not match. DNA is genetic material found in the nucleus of every cell and is unique for each person. It is found in body fluids such as blood, sweat, and saliva.

Everyone was hopeful that DNA might finally solve the Zodiac case. If it could be collected from the back of stamps that the Zodiac had licked, it could be compared to DNA from various suspects. All were aware, however, that the evidence was very old, and the DNA might be degraded to the point that it was impossible to use.

In 2002 a usable amount of DNA was finally collected off the back of a stamp. When compared, however, it did not

In 2002, investigators hoped that DNA testing could help solve the Zodiac case. However, nothing has been uncovered yet.

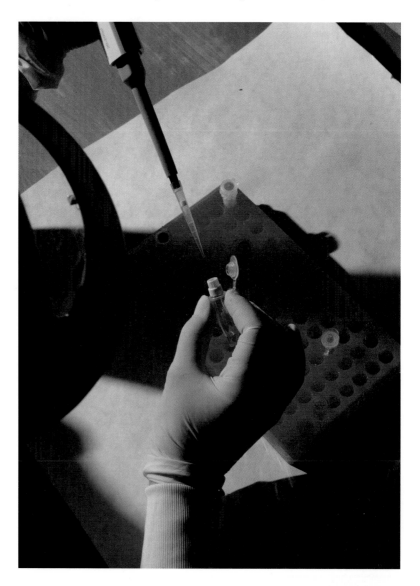

Still Difficult

Decades have passed since the Zodiac attacks, but victims' families still suffer. Pam Huckabee cannot forget that her sister, Darlene Ferrin, was murdered on the Fourth of July in 1969, and explains her feelings in journalist Rich Freedman's article "Reliving a Nightmare," published in the Vallejo Times-Herald in 2007.

Though it's been nearly 38 years, [Pam] Huckabee said the family still finds it difficult—"though it's getting easier"—to celebrate Independence Day.

"The Fourth of July was the favorite holiday for our family," she said. "We'd always look forward to going to Blue Rock Springs [Park]."

"I still get calls on July 4: 'Pam, are you OK?'" Huckabee said. "There's not enough paper to write about how this has affected us."

After Ferrin was killed, "it took a while to sink in," [Ferrin's brother Leo] Suennen said. "I see her one day, and she's gone the next. Fourth of July for me is still real depressing. It's still bad."

Rich Freedman, "Reliving a Nightmare," *Times-Herald* (Vallejo, CA), February 26, 2007.

match any suspect. In February 2007, Vallejo police sent three more letters allegedly written by the killer to the crime lab for testing. Again, the results were disappointing. Vallejo police spokesman Rick Nichelman tried to sound hopeful: "The initial testing is complete, and they didn't yield anything. But there's still a chance something could be found with new tests [in the future]."[96]

Still at Large

Even the most up-to-date methods of catching the Zodiac had failed. The killer, if he was still alive, was still at large. The thought was depressing, but those who pursued him refused to admit defeat. They insisted that there was always the possibility of someday identifying him. Napa County Sheriff's detective Kenneth Narlow states, "As time goes by, I have my doubts that the Zodiac is still alive. But I still think the case can be solved."[97]

Solving it will require hard evidence, something that puts all the questions, suspicions, and theories to rest. Perhaps a deathbed confession will lead to an answer. Perhaps a family will discover an incriminating black hood while going through a dead relative's belongings. Or there are other possibilities. "If the case is to be solved it will be done by a reader, a witness, or some suspect seeking to clear his conscience, answer all our questions, and write the end of the Zodiac mystery,"[98] states journalist Michael Butterfield.

No matter what the ending, the Zodiac case has gone down in history as an example of the power of the written word to influence, to mislead, and to create panic. It also demonstrates how a single man's twisted desire for recognition led to the disruption and devastation of countless lives. Profiler Gregg O. McCrary sums it up: "Ultimately, I think, for Zodiac, these crimes were about getting notoriety. . . . That was as much of the thrill for him, perhaps more, than any other part of the incidents. . . . fame and a sense of superiority were probably more exciting to him than the violence itself. He just wanted to be known as a notorious killer It was probably the only thing he ever accomplished."[99]

Notes

Introduction: "This Is the Zodiac Speaking"

1. Zodiac letter, received August 4, 1969. Zodiackiller.com. www.zodiackiller.com/ZLetter1.html.

2. Quoted in Charles Russo, "Zodiac: The Killer Who Will Not Die," *San Francisco* (magazine), March 2007. www.sanfran.com/archives/view_story/1531.

3. Quoted in Russo, "Zodiac."

4. Quoted in Matthias Gafni, "Still a Suspect," *Times–Herald* (Vallejo, CA), October 15, 2002.

5. Quoted in Dixie Reid, "'60s Killings Are Still a Bizarre Whodunit," *Sacramento Bee*, February 28, 2007.

Chapter 1: Good-bye, Young Lovers

6. Quoted in Napa County Sheriff's Department interview with Bryan Calvin Hartnell, September 28, 1969. Zodiackiller.com. www.zodiackiller.com/HartnellInterview7.html.

7. Quoted in Tom Voigt, "The Lake Herman Tragedy," Zodiackiller.com, December 20, 2003. www.zodiackiller.com/LHR2.html.

8. Quoted in Michael Taylor, "Undying Legend of a Killer," *San Francisco Chronicle*, March 1, 2007.

9. Quoted in Voigt, "The Lake Herman Tragedy."

10. Quoted in Vallejo Police Department crime report, July 5, 1969. Zodiackiller.com. www.zodiackiller.com/DFR6.html.

11. Quoted in Vallejo Police Department crime report, July 5, 1969. Zodiackiller.com. www.zodiackiller.com/DFR4.html.

12. Quoted in Napa County Sheriff's Department interview with Bryan Calvin Hartnell. Zodiackiller.com. www.zodiackiller.com/HartnellInterview2.html.

13. Quoted in Napa County Sheriff's Department crime report, September 28, 1969. Zodiackiller.com. www.zodiackiller.com/LBReport23.html.

14. Quoted in Napa County Sheriff's Department interview with Bryan Calvin Hartnell. Zodiackiller.com. www.zodiackiller.com/HartnellInterview7.html.

15. Quoted in Selicia Kennedy-Ross, "Area Man Survived After Zodiac Tried to Kill Him," *Inland Valley Daily Bulletin* (Ontario, CA), February 24, 2007.

16. Quoted in Santa Barbara County Sheriff Department press release, 1972. Zodiackiller.com. www.zodiackiller.com/SBPressRelease.html.

17. Kathleen Johns letter, postmarked July 24, 1970. Zodiackiller.com. www.zodiackiller.com/JohnsLetter.html.

18. Pines postcard, received March 22, 1971. Zodiackiller.com. www.zodiackiller.com/PinesCard.html.

19. Quoted in Robert Graysmith, *Zodiac*. New York: Berkeley Books, 2007, p. 178.

20. Gregg O. McCrary, "Profile of the Zodiac Killer," CrimeLibrary.com, 2007. www.crimelibrary.com/serial_killers/notorious/zodiac_profile/5.html.

Chapter 2: Taunts from the Killer

21. Napa County Sheriff Department crime report." Zodiackiller.com. www.zodiackiller.com/LBReport16.html.

22. Quoted in ABC News, "Primetime Live: The Hunt for the Zodiac Killer," October 17, 2002. http://members.aol.com/ZArchives/primetime.html.

23. Quoted in Russo, "Zodiac."

24. Zodiac letter, received August 1, 1969. Zodiackiller.com. www.zodiackiller.com/ChronicleLetter1.html.

25. Zodiac letter. Zodiackiller.com. www.zodiackiller.com/ChronicleLetter2.html.

26. Zodiac letter, received August 4, 1969. Zodiackiller.com. www.zodiackiller.com/ZLetter3.html.

27. Stine letter, received October 14, 1969. Zodiackiller.com. www.zodiackiller.com/StineLetter.html.

28. Quoted in Graysmith, *Zodiac*, p. 104.

29. Stine letter.

30. Stine letter.

31. Quoted in Russo, "Zodiac."

32. Zodiac letter, received November 9, 1969. Zodiackiller.com. www.zodiackiller.com/BombLetter4.html.

33. Zodiac letter, received November 9, 1969.

34. Quoted in Tim Reiters, "Expert Frustrated; Handwriting's Not on Wall for Zodiac," *Examiner* (San Francisco, CA) January 30, 1978. http://foia.fbi.gov/zodiac/zodiac5.pdf.

35. Quoted in Graysmith, *Zodiac*, p. 160.

36. Quoted in Reiters, "Expert Frustrated."

37. Quoted in Reiters, "Expert Frustrated."

38. Bates letter, postmarked April 30, 1967. Zodiackiller.com. www.zodiackiller.com/BatesLetter1.html.

39. Zodiac letter, postmarked March 13, 1971. Zodiackiller.com. www.zodiackiller.com/LATimesLetter.html.

40. Quoted in Jake Wark, "Final Letters," CrimeLibrary.com. www.crimelibrary.com/serial_killers/notorious/zodiac/25.html.

41. Quoted in *San Francisco Chronicle*, "A 'Murder Code' Broken," *San Francisco Chronicle*, August 2, 1969.

42. Richard Connell, "The Most Dangerous Game." Classic Short Stories, 2007. www.classicshorts.com/stories/danger.html.

43. Quoted in Graysmith, *Zodiac*, p. 61.

44. Michael D. Kelleher and David Van Nuys, *This Is the Zodiac Speaking: Into the Mind of a Serial Killer*. Westport, CT: Praeger, 2002, pp. 130–31.

45. Kelleher and Van Nuys, *This Is the Zodiac Speaking*, pp. 100–101.

Chapter 3: Hunting the Zodiac

46. Quoted in Taylor, "Undying Legend of a Killer."

47. Quoted in Marsha Dorgan, "Tracking the Mark of the Zodiac for Decades," *Napa Valley Register*, February 18, 2007. www.napavalleyregister.com/articles/2007/02/18/news/local/iq_3821597.txt.

48. Quoted in *JIVE Magazine*, *Zodiac* movie review, *JIVE Magazine*, March 1, 2007. www.jivemagazine.com/review.php?rid=2247.

49. Quoted in Graysmith, *Zodiac*, p. 38.

50. Quoted in Graysmith, *Zodiac*, p. 77.

51. Vallejo Police Department crime report. www.zodiackiller.com/DFR10.html

52. Quoted in Graysmith, *Zodiac*, p. 78.

53. Donald Fouke, San Francisco Police Department intra-departmental memorandum, November 12, 1969. Zodiackiller.com. www.zodiackiller.com/FoukeReport.html.

54. Quoted in Graysmith, *Zodiac*, p. 123.

55. Quoted in Russo, "Zodiac."

56. Halloween card, postmarked October 27, 1970. Zodiackiller.com. www.zodiackiller.com/HalloweenCard.html.

57. Duffy Jennings, "Zodiac vs. the Chron City Desk," *San Francisco Chronicle*, February 25, 2007. http://sfgate.com/cgi-bin/article.cgi?f=/c/a/2007/02/25/PKGANO4TRF1.DTL.

Chapter 4: Strange and Suspicious

58. Quoted in Graysmith, *Zodiac*, p. 67.

59. Quoted in Graysmith, *Zodiac*, p. 78.

60. McCrary, "Profile of the Zodiac Killer."

61. Quoted in Taylor, "Undying Legend of a Killer."

62. Zodiac Killer Facts, "Mt. Diablo and Radian Theory," Zodiac Killer Facts (Web site), 2007. www.zodiackillerfacts.com/radian.htm.

63. Quoted in *JIVE Magazine*, *Zodiac* movie review.

64. McCrary, "Profile of the Zodiac Killer."

65. Quoted in Lance Williams, "Zodiac's Written Clues Fascinate Document Expert," *San Francisco Chronicle*, March 3, 2007.

66. Quoted in *Redding Record Searchlight*, "Author Claims Zodiac Killer Was His Brother," *Redding Record Searchlight* (Redding, CA), November 1, 1991.

67. Quoted in R.V. Sheide, "The Zodiac Is Back . . . But Did He Ever Leave?" newsreview.com, March 8, 2007. www.newsreview.com/reno/Content?oid=291925.

68. Harvey Hines, "Summary of Facts," 1976. ZodiacKiller.com. www.zodiackiller.com/KaneReport10.html.

69. Quoted in Rider McDowell, "On the Trail of the Zodiac," May 8–15, 1994. www.zodiackiller.com/KH10.html

70. Quoted in McDowell, "On the Trail of the Zodiac." www.zodiackiller.com/KH15.html.

71. Quoted in Graysmith, *Zodiac*, p. 285.

72. Quoted in Zodiac Killer Facts, "Arthur Lee Allen = Primed Suspect," 2007. Zodiac Killer Facts (Web site). www.zodiackillerfacts.com/allen.htm.

73. Quoted in Simon Read, "Zodiac's Shadow Crossed Valley," *Alameda Times-Star* (Alameda, CA), March 13, 2005.

Chapter 5: Going Nowhere

74. Quoted in Rich Freedman, "The First Zodiac Attack," *Times-Herald* (Vallejo, CA), February 27, 2007.

75. Quoted in Russo, "Zodiac."

76. Quoted in Tom Voigt, "The Murder of Cheri Jo Bates," Zodiackiller.com, October 30, 2003. www.zodiackiller.com/BatesUpdate2.html.

77. Quoted in Graysmith, *Zodiac*, p. 178.

78. Quoted in Williams, "Zodiac's Written Clues Fascinate Document Expert."

79. Quoted in Graysmith, *Zodiac*, p. 207.

80. Quoted in Andrew Curtin and Larry D. Hatfield, "New Puzzles Further Muddle Zodiac Case," *Examiner* (San Francisco, CA), July 11, 1978.

81. Quoted in Curtin and Hatfield, "New Puzzles Further Muddle Zodiac Case."

82. Quoted in Curtin and Hatfield, "New Puzzles Further Muddle Zodiac Case."

83. Quoted in Lisa O'Neill Hill, "Mystery Kept Alive: The Work of Amateur Sleuths Fascinated with a 1966 Riverside Death—Possibly at the Hands of the Zodiac Serial Killer—Inspires a Documentary," *Press-Enterprise* (Riverside, CA), May 13, 2002.

84. Quoted in Richard Freedman, "The Zodiac Fascination," *Times-Herald* (Vallejo, CA), July 1, 2002.

85. Graysmith, *Zodiac*, p. 48.

86. Quoted in Jim Okerblom, "'Zodiac Killer' Uncaught Despite Tantalizing Clues," *San Diego Union*, April 4, 1987.

87. Quoted in Margie Boule, "Portlander Is Obsessed by Serial Killer—and He's Not Alone," *Oregonian* (Portland, OR), July 28, 2002.

88. Zodiac letter, postmarked July 26, 1970. Zodiackiller.com. www.zodiackiller.com/Mikado1.html.

89. Curt Rowlett, "Z Files: Case Overview," Labyrinth13 (Web site), 1999. http://labyrinth13.com/ZFiles_overview.htm.

90. Zodiackiller.com, "Zodiac Suspect: Michael O'Hare." Zodiackiller.com. www.zodiackiller.com/SuspectOHare.html.

91. Quoted in Russo, "Zodiac."

Chapter 6: Beyond the Zodiac Murders

92. Quoted in *JIVE Magazine*, *Zodiac* movie review.

93. Quoted in Kennedy-Ross, "Area Man Survived After Zodiac Tried to Kill Him."

94. Quoted in Tom Hays, "Trademark Symbol Led Police to an Arrest in Zodiac Killings," *Boston Globe*, June 20, 1996.

95. Quoted in Eric Talmadge, "Similarities Found Between Japan Slaying, Zodiac Killer," *Seattle Times*, June 4, 1997.

96. Quoted in Rachel Raskin-Zrihen, "So Far, DNA Tests Turn Up Nothing New on Zodiac, *Times-Herald* (Vallejo, CA), May 25, 2007.

97. Quoted in Zodiac Killer Facts, "A Case Summary of the Zodiac Killer," Zodiac Killer Facts (Web site), 2007. www.zodiackillerfacts.com/case.htm.

98. Michael Butterfield, "The Zodiac Movie: Fact vs. Fincher," Zodiac Killer Facts (Web site), February 2007. www.zodiackillerfacts.com/blog.

99. McCrary, "Profile of the Zodiac Killer." www.crimelibrary.com/serial_killers/notorious/zodiac_profile/6.html.

For More Information

Books

Robert Graysmith, *Zodiac*. New York: Berkeley Books, 1996. A complete and mostly accurate account of the Zodiac case by the former *San Francisco Chronicle* political cartoonist who followed the case as it unfolded.

Robert Graysmith, *Zodiac Unmasked*. New York: Berkeley Books, 2002. In this sequel to *Zodiac*, Graysmith makes the case that Arthur Leigh Allen is the infamous killer.

Internet Sources

Richard Connell, "The Most Dangerous Game." Classic Short Stories, 1924. www.classicshorts.com/stories/danger.html.

Federal Bureau of Investigation, "Zodiac Killer," Federal Bureau of Investigation, 2007. http://foia.fbi.gov/foiaindex/zodiac.htm.

Gregg McCrary, "Profile of the Zodiac Killer," CrimeLibrary.com, 2007. www.crimelibrary.com/serial_killers/notorious/zodiac_profile/1_index.html.

Charles Russo, "Zodiac: The Killer Who Will Not Die," *San Francisco* (magazine), March 2007. www.sanfran.com/archives/view_story/1531.

Jake Wark, "The Zodiac Killer," CrimeLibrary.com, 2007. www.crimelibrary.com/serial_killers/notorious/zodiac/river_1.html.

Web Sites

"This Is the Zodiac Speaking . . ." (http://members.aol.com/Jakewark). This site, created by Jake Wark, reports the thoughts and theories of independent researchers and provides archived media and news reports and additional sources for further study.

Zodiackiller.com (www.zodiackiller.com). Zodiac enthusiast Tom Voigt's site contains complete information about the Zodiac case, including police reports and photos, letters and ciphers, overviews of victims and suspects, a message board, and more.

Zodiac Killer Facts (www.zodiackillerfacts.com). Another great Zodiac site. Discusses the facts as well as Zodiac theories and legends. Contains links to other sites.

Index

Picture Credits

About the Author

Diane Yancey lives in the Pacific Northwest with her husband, Michael; their dog, Gelato; and their cats, Lily, Newton, and Alice. Yancey has written more than thirty-five books for middle-grade and high school readers, including *The Case of the Green River Killer* and *The Unabomber*.